Toxic News?
Covering Climate Change

Edited by John Mair, John Ryley, and Andrew Beck

Toxic News?
Covering Climate Change

Edited by John Mair, John Ryley, and Andrew Beck

Cover by

Dean Stockton

Published by Bite-Sized Books Ltd 2023

Bite-Sized Books Limited
16 High Holborn, London, WC1V 6BX England
Registered in the UK. Company Registration
No: 9395379

ISBN: 978-1-7395253-4-7

CONTENTS

Acknowledgements

Never accept a drink from John Ryley in an Oxford pub with plenty of beer. It leads to books like these. A balmy summer evening in the Harcourt Arms in Jericho, chewing the cud, and out pops this very timely book. An audit of the febrile and fast-moving world of climate change reporting in British media, it examines the issue from a range of perspectives and in a variety of contexts, ranging from London streets, to British politics, and to the global stage of COPs.

First off, big thanks to JR for the idea and his unstinting support for the project. It could not have been done without him. Equal kudos to Andrew Beck: pedantic, finickity, and precise. But both JR and JM need an Andrew. Thanks also to our publisher Julian Costley of Bite-Sized Books. We hope this will be another BSB best seller. As ever, graphic genius Dean Stockton has enhanced the product with a brilliant and meaningful cover.

But most of all thanks to the twenty-four contributors. They write against deadline for no fee and have to survive my constant chivvying. They are the true heroes.

Finally, a big hug to our long-suffering partners. Late nights and early mornings taking up family space must be annoying. They have shown huge patience.

John Mair, Oxford, England, October 2023

The editors

John Mair was born in the then-British Guiana (to an 'Old Guianese' mother: heritage not age) in 1950. He went to Sacred Heart RC School, in Georgetown. John won the top scholarship in the Common Entrance examination in Guiana in 1961. Then his parents emigrated to the UK. He returns regularly to Guyana. He writes there under the *nom de guerre* Bill Cotton/Reform. John is the proud owner of a Guyana UK High Commission Award. He attended the LSE, Sussex, and Leeds universities. John has taught journalism at the universities of Coventry, Kent, Northampton, Brunel, Edinburgh Napier, and Guyana and at the Communication University of China. He has edited more than fifty hackademic volumes over the last twelve years. His most recent books have been on Inspector Morse in Oxford, ten Oxford authors, reporting the war in Ukraine, and Boris Johnson's time as UK Prime Minister. In a previous life, he was an award-winning producer/director for the BBC, ITV, and Channel 4, and a secondary school teacher.

John Ryley was the Editor-in-Chief of Sky News from 2006 to 2023. He was a BBC graduate trainee, then a programme editor of ITV's *News at Ten*, before joining Sky News. In 2021, The Royal Television Society gave him the Outstanding Contribution award for journalism. The judges said 'he has effected genuine change in our business [...] his style is innovative, idiosyncratic. His integrity, influence, and authority, colossal'. He is a trustee of the NCTJ, and will become Chair of the Geddes Trust in March 2024.

Andrew Beck worked in UK secondary, further, and higher education for forty-two years, lastly as International Partnership Manager for Coventry University's Faculty of Arts and Humanities. He is author of oft-cited books such as *Cultural Work* and *Communication Studies: The Essential Introduction*, as well as having served as chief examiner for public and professional examinations in Communication. Retired from full-time work he continues to teach at and advise international universities, as well as researching and publishing on a range of media issues. Recent publications include contributions to, and co-editing books on Covid-19, the Ukraine war, Boris Johnson's premiership, as well as occasional features for *China Eye*.

SECTION ONE

Stormy weather

Preface

Tom Heap makes a plea for the climate change story to be told like other stories

If the story of our struggle to halt climate change were a play or film script, I think we'd be at the end of act two: we now know how to slay the beast but the will to do so is in danger of ebbing away. The pain of the fight is immediate while the prize remains distant. The outcome is in real jeopardy. It could go either way.

Climate related disasters and dire warnings from scientists continue apace, but they are familiar now, prompting few headlines and even fewer policy moves. There is a shocking political vacuum surrounding climate change. While the UK government signals indifference or hostility to effective carbon cutting action, the opposition parties show limited enthusiasm for talking about how the world needs saving and this is how they are planning to do it. How has it come to this and is journalism letting politicians get away with it?

Why does it matter?

The push to stop burning stuff is now affecting people's lives: the phasing out of gas boilers and petrol or diesel cars, and city redesign to encourage cycling or walking. Though, in the grand sweep of civilisation,

I would argue these are tweaks not huge wrenches, they do cause anguish, both amplified and validated by a cost-of-living crisis. This is a 'good' (in the journalistic sense), relatively new, human interest story. But it's not the only story. Remember that one about the passing of the 2008 Climate Change Act, which received overwhelming support from all political parties, and wide support beyond, the story that limiting climate change was an existential struggle and we'd all play some part in it? Where is the political leadership to say, 'We know this is a big deal. We know it'll involve some change and discomfort for you. But there are opportunities too and here is how we're going to manage the change with speed and equity'. And why are political reporters virtually silent on this void?

There is so little evidence that the public actively reject green policies; generally, polls suggest support. If you phrase the climate action question and add 'if it costs you money' backing drops. (See Chapter 7 'Mind the gap: public attitudes towards climate change'.) Of course it does. The same is true if you ask about defence or policing: 'Do you want it to be strong?' 'Yes.' 'Do you want to pay a lot for that'? 'Err …'

On 20 September 2023 Prime Minister Rishi Sunak announced plans to water down some policies to fight climate change. With some pretty tortuous logic he argued that putting off meaningful actions showed that he was honest and serious about cutting carbon. Then came the truly bizarre section where he announced the scrapping of policies that weren't actually policies: frequent flyer taxes, obligatory car sharing, seven bins, meat tax plans. I did a live interview on Sky News that night trying to highlight this absurdity of creating false demons just to vanquish them, without saying he was lying – a red light word. I just about managed it but clearly Twitter (X) users thought the sight of me teetering on the edge was revelatory as 120,000 views of a one-minute clip testify. So where does balance and bias lie in covering climate change?

My employers are tolerant - thankfully

I am very lucky. Unlike some contributors to this book, with the BBC and Sky, I have never worked for a proprietor who is pushing a denialist line. I reckon I am allowed to be biased towards saving the planet. Though I do wonder if education correspondents consider themselves biased towards better education or business correspondents towards thriving business. In June 2007 the BBC Trust published *From seesaw to wagon wheel – a report into impartiality in the 21st century,* where it stated the broadcaster didn't need to give airtime to deniers on the atmospheric physics of climate change as, given the strong scientific consensus, this would be 'false balance'.

Once you accept that it's happening, it's hard to avoid the logic that something should be done, even if much of the media sees that truth as 'old hat'.

Sewage in the water; big issue, easy outrage

One environmental issue is swamping the media today – water. Rivers and seas are polluted with human excrement. I have little doubt that the water companies and government regulators have mismanaged our supply and sewage system and should be held to account. But every bandwagon comes with an alarm bell. This is a story with easy villains: greedy water companies, yucky pictures, and, perhaps most importantly, little need for the audience to adapt their own lifestyles beside turning off the tap when brushing your teeth.

It's easy outrage. Climate is hard.

Climate change is – or should be – the most gripping story around. The stakes could not be higher, there are some heroes, and we are all players. So why are the two Cs - climate change - often an audience turn off, whether in print or broadcast?

Much of the time, the climate change article will leave the listener or reader feeling guilty, miserable, and powerless. These are not enjoyable sensations and, consciously or not, we often seek to avoid repeating them. Viewer figures for the Attenborough documentary episode on how we are destroying nature are lower than those for the uncomplicated marvels that went before. This feel-bad trinity is almost unique to the subject. We may feel sad about the grinding war in Yemen but it is not our fault. We may feel angry about the state of the NHS but we have some influence on national health policy through voting and our own health through behaviour. We can just 'enjoy' being horrified by true crime or thrilled by stunning scientific breakthroughs.

How most people feel about climate change

The public are not a homogenous mass in the way they receive climate related stories. Some just lap them up and just want them screamed louder to validate their own views and to bludgeon opponents. At the other end, there is a small number who deny the threat exists at all and think it's all a vested interest conspiracy. I am most interested in the big lump in the middle. A legacy of a professional life, spent mostly in the centrist BBC, has left me with the belief that, despite the atomising infection of social media, there is still a general audience to be engaged in climate stories.

But how to do this . . . that's the trick. One that I try to pull off on BBC Radio 4, *Countryfile* and, most recently, my climate show on Sky News. I probably frequently fail. I once had a stand-up row in a group meeting with a BBC commissioner who insisted that people wanted to know 'what *they* can do', a green echo of the once in vogue phrase 'News you can use'.

I have my doubts. Principally because it takes the journalist straight to the pulpit (a place with an enormously powerful tractor beam in the green universe) yet people don't like being preached to. When surveys ask 'would you like more information about what you can do for the climate crisis?' people tend to say 'Yes', just like they tell canvassers they believe in high welfare pork before going into the supermarket to buy the cheapest sausages.

The climate change story and how to tell it

The answer is to treat it just like any other story and use all the same techniques: breaking news, great access, human triumph and tragedy, revelation, celebrity, humour, amazing pictures. This may sound achingly obvious but is often forgotten when the justification that it is a story we 'ought' to do, can make us lazy in *how* we tell it.

In 2021 I wrote a book celebrating climate change solutions that span out of the Radio 4 series *39 Ways to Save the Planet.* I wanted Arnold Schwarzenegger to write the foreword, not solely for film fanboy reasons but because he could appeal across a broad spectrum and not just to the converted. During his time as state governor, he delivered huge cuts in California's carbon emissions, made a real difference to climate change, and he still continues to campaign But he is about as far from a sermonising monk as you can get. In the event, he wrote the foreword and did a great broadcast interview.

One of his key thoughts is: 'Don't call it climate change, call it pollution. *No-one* likes pollution, whereas the term 'climate change' is divisive, and excess CO2 *is* a pollutant.'

Arnie still lives a pretty high consumption lifestyle and is an easy target for the charge of hypocrisy. 'Hypocrisy' and its close cousin 'greenwash' are favourite villains on the climate change beat. Much of this is fine and valid journalism. After all emissions will only be reduced by actions not claims. But sometimes I feel it punishes those who try but don't completely succeed while ignoring those who do nothing. I want companies and those with influence to do more green stuff and I am happy for them to get public kudos for boasting about what they've done. It is an incentive to do more. But mistakes will be made and then the 'Gotcha!' story will play big. Meanwhile 'Acme Evil Corp' pollutes constantly, never tries not to, and rarely gets a mention. I don't have a prescription here, it's more of an observation.

But it's worth remembering, when it comes to climate action and covering it, none of us has the monopoly of virtue.

About the contributor

Tom Heap has reported on climate and environment for nearly 25 years, mostly on the BBC with the *News, Countryfile, Panorama*, and *Costing the Earth* on Radio 4. For the last year he has also been presenting *The Climate Show with Tom Heap* on Sky News, where he actually began his broadcasting career as a sound man. In 2021 he published the upbeat climate change solutions book *39 Ways to Save the Planet* (BBC Books), and is currently writing a book on smart land use.

Introduction

Heat kills but it's not a popular headline

One fact cannot be disputed: extreme heat kills. Climate coverage is not popular with TV audiences. But **John Ryley** argues impartiality can be an editorial trap

"I read somewhere that the sun's getting hotter every year," said Tom genially. It seems that pretty soon the earth's going to fall into the sun - or wait a minute - it's just the opposite - the sun's getting colder every year," says the confused but assertive Tom Buchanan in F Scott Fitzgerald's satirical Jazz Age novel *The Great Gatsby* on an especially hot late summer New York afternoon in the early 1920s. Precisely one hundred years later the public, scientists, and journalists are all still confused by climate change and disagree, sometimes vehemently, about the causes and solutions to climate change as wildfires, floods, and searing heat strike the planet. Yet one fact cannot be disputed: extreme heat kills and kills quickly, kills the earth's plants, wildlife, and fish as well. It is an existential threat, a highly significant story. Political leaders, too, disagree about how to best to tackle the problem of fast rising temperatures and some want to slow down the march towards net zero. After a quiet summer of news in 2023 broadcast, print, and social media in Britain focused on the Prime Minister's U-turn on measures to combat global warming and pollution ahead of a General Election. Voters realising the move away from fossil fuels is expensive don't want to pay the cost of replacing their gas boilers with heat pumps or getting rid of their aging petrol or diesel cars. Mr Sunak's policy change was leaked to the licence fee funded BBC, a one-hundred-year-old news organisation that climate sceptics believe has totally abandoned its critical commitment to the principle of strict impartiality, the public service's sine qua non, when it reports on climate change.

Question the evidence to establish the facts

My view is impartiality can be a supine, editorial trap: journalists should question the evidence - scientists' data, academics' research, sceptics' views, communities' testimony, video - and rigorously pursue the truth to establish the facts. To assay. On my watch Sky News saw the rapid heating up of the planet as a relevant and significant story for our audiences. During my seventeen years as the boss, I was very clear on the position Sky News should take. Speaking at the COP26 conference in Glasgow in 2022, I outlined boldly our editorial approach. I said, "Climate change exists. It is a threat to our planet. And we believe that it is indeed a crisis - a crisis that our audiences expect us to report with robust rigour." I said there were few stories that were as urgent and compelling as the climate crisis. Sky wanted to ensure that our audiences knew the facts and the human stories so that they could fully understand what is going on. "This meant," I continued, "not just reporting what is happening right now. It also meant reporting on the reality of the future of our planet and the attempts to prevent global warming." I told the Glasgow audience how Sky News was proud of its environmental heritage: how Sky had campaigned to save the rainforest from 2006; how Sky News had campaigned in 2017, before the BBC, to remove single-use plastic; how it had appointed in 2019 the first dedicated climate change reporter in UK broadcasting, Hannah Thomas-Peter; how it brought its audiences climate stories every single day on *The Daily Climate Show* launched in 2021, the U.K's first dedicated daily climate news programme; and how it had set up a special COP26 pop-up channel to broadcast the conference's daily proceedings. I made clear, "We would evaluate the evidence with an open mind then we tell our audiences what the facts are and clearly explain the implications. Providing the facts does not mean having both sides to debate whether climate change exists. Because it does exist. The only debate is about what can be done and how soon and who by." The speech ended with this peroration: "Sky News is proud to take the lead on the environment because we see it an essential ingredient of the service we provide [...] And we will show that journalism can be a force for good."

Climate TV news coverage unpopular

Adamantine rhetoric that the COP26 conference attendees applauded loudly. But the focus on climate news and bespoke programming wasn't popular away from Glasgow. It wasn't popular with the news desk who needed frequent reminders that climate change matters, that there was more to the news than just crime, bullets, and Westminster gossip. They replied they had heard it all before: the top line - the earth is heating up - is not new. It wasn't popular with our audiences: climate news always ranks high in what people consider important and should be reported, but people don't engage it with as much as they claim in opinion polls. The highly produced *Daily Climate Show* held an audience, but it was a small in size compared to the audiences watching the news before and after the programme. Sky News saw its audiences fall by nearly a third on average when the *Daily Climate Show* was broadcast compared to the previous slot - a non-stop news programme - only for the audiences to rise again once the show was over. Climate documentaries on Sky News have tended to fare a little better with some showings seeing big audience engagement and numbers but they are rare moments. For example, ' Climate Crisis', a documentary about the impact of flooding on Bangladesh in 2021 on Sky News reached more than 2.47m people - a figure that matches what the terrestrial channels would expect for highly produced documentary style climate coverage. And the labour intensive, much promoted COP26 special pop-up channel got next to no viewing even in Sky homes. Chastening. Essentially any coverage of the climate story needs to be done in a documentary format to really see any significant cut through with viewers. On top of that it wasn't popular with my sharp successor, Jonathan Levy, who within a month of taking over in May 2023 had dropped the *Daily Climate Show*, though not the weekly edition presented by Tom Heap. Jonathan argued that “Man-made climate change is indisputable - it’s settled. But what we do about it is not settled at all and subject to an increasingly broad and vigorous debate which Sky News must reflect. I felt the *Daily Climate Show* – which served Sky News very well when it was launched around COP26 – was by now constraining and marginalising our climate coverage and instead wanted it to be a much more regular feature of our daily journalism." A good point which is echoed by the Reuters Institute for the Study of Journalism that believes climate journalism should encompass reporting on every facet of life - everything from sport to food and not operate in a vertical silo. It's worth noting that the Reuters Institute run a ground-breaking, virtual course aimed at reporters and media executives around the world - The Oxford Climate Journalism Network - to try to make climate journalism better. "Every story," they say, "is a climate story."

No 'official' line

The offer to write a piece for this timely book has not been popular with the climate sceptics. Its editors set out to offer a broad range of views yet persuading the sceptics to take part has been hard. One well known, outspoken newspaper columnist, said he 'would rather discuss English linguistic philosophy whilst having root canal treatment'. Robin Aitken, a former BBC correspondent turned spikey *Daily Telegraph* writer, has thankfully sat in the dentist's chair armed with his keyboard. In this book he says he doesn't know if the 'climate doom mongers' are right or wrong but believes the British media, particularly the broadcasters, have reported the climate crisis 'very badly'. He says groupthink is to blame, arguing there is no debate on climate change which has led to a lack of scrutiny over government policy. I say Robin is wrong. He is wrong to suggest broadcasters have taken an ‘official’ line. Unlike newspapers, broadcast newsrooms are polylithic structures whose journalism reflects a broad range of their employees’ views. Day after day Sky News would interview a wide spectrum of interviewees - scientists, residents, sceptics, politicians, academics - with different viewpoints on how to handle climate change. He is wrong to suggest the coverage is more like ‘an ad campaign than proper journalism’. To question and assess the evidence with an open mind is at the heart of good journalism, often with reporters on the ground. Our coverage was not selling a product, it was reporting what our journalists witnessed. The ultra-competitive rival broadcast organisations haven't all got together to take part in a joint movement. He is wrong to suggest there is ‘too little scepticism’ about climate change: the Sky newsroom is full of independently minded individuals unwillingly to accept a narrative, keen to hear a range of opinions. In recent years many climate sceptics have been interviewed by Sky News including, for example, the Danish author Bjorn Lomborg who was a panellist on a 2020 special live programme 'Climate After Covid: A Green Recovery?'. At the time he also wrote an opinion piece for the Sky News website making clear his position, 'Climate alarm leads to anxious lives and bad policies. It also takes our attention off the world's many other problems like preparing for global pandemics. We can do so much better'. Robin is right to assert the first duty of journalism is to bring about the widest possible debate on the big policy issues. It takes two people to debate, and I acknowledge that sometimes the 'climatetari' have been unwilling to take part in a debate with an interviewee they perceive as a 'sceptic'. I also accept predicting exactly what will happen because of climate change is imprecise. But the idea of there being 'sides' on the existence of human driven climate change and the extent of the damage it has wrought so far is outdated. Even the fossil fuel companies have ditched it in favour of their delaying tactics.

Question everything

This book contains rare insights from people who influence or have influenced public opinion. Tony Blair's chief Prime Ministerial speech writer, Philip Collins, who pioneered the analysis of major speeches, looks at how world leaders have tried to communicate the danger of climate change. He asks why there have been no memorable speeches, in his words 'great', about the subject. The likes of Richard Nixon and Margaret Thatcher in the 1970s and 1980s tried to address the problem but their keynote words didn't stick. He concludes, 'nobody is in charge and speeches come alive when the speaker can promise meaningful action'. A sober thought.

The journalist Matthew d'Ancona accuses Rushi Sunak of applying the same approach to climate change as he did to Brexit. He says the prime minister is instinctively suspicious of green commitments as yet another regulatory imposition upon the free market by the state. He compares the campaign for the UK to leave Europe with the campaign to scrap the country's commitment to net zero with Nigel Farage leading the charge for a referendum on emission targets. Both ideologies, Matthew says, 'share a distaste for “experts” – economists in the case of Brexit, the world’s scientists in the case of climate change’.

The doyen of pollsters, Professor John Curtice, offers a fascinating insight into public opinion. Most people in Britain are concerned about climate change, he says. Almost eight out of 10 say they are ‘very’ or ‘fairly’ concerned in an Ipsos survey from July 2023. But he suggests some proposals for reducing carbon emissions are more popular than others, leaving scope for the issue to become divisive at election time. Not least of the reasons for the difference between people’s level of concern and their attitudes towards implementation is their reluctance to pay for the costs of transition.

In a salient piece, ‘Is Fleet Street in climate denial?’, former *Times* Night Editor, Liz Gerard, describes how twenty years ago she was taken to task, given, in her words, ‘a full-scale carpeting’, for rewriting the splash headline about global warming to make clear climate change was man-made. But the paper's proprietor Rupert Murdoch thought otherwise. She laments a lack of analysis of environmental stories by today’s print media and concludes, ‘Our newspapers are out of touch, out of date, and out of ideas’.

Ted Young, one of Britain's most successful tabloid journalists, once a *Sun* headline writer, more recently the editor of the *Metro*, in a racy broadside, attacks the hypocrisy of world leaders from presidents to royalty for the way they preach to people on the environment remarking, ‘It was a bit rich when Prince Harry attended the Google Camp in Sicily back in 2019 after flying in by private jet to preach to us all, barefoot on a beach, about saving the planet'. He champions the right of journalists to question and challenge the accepted narrative: 'The press is right to question everything. What is the cost of shifting from using fossil fuel to electricity? Or indeed the cost of not doing this in the long term […] Because you ask these questions, does not mean you are a swivel-eyed reactionary'.

Several front lines have developed in climate journalism. Recent years have seen an increase in protests by organisations such as Extinction Rebellion (XR) and Just Stop Oil. One video journalist who reports up close on the tactics of climate activists is Zoe Broughton. Her work focuses on what she calls 'the greatest threat our humanity has faced - that of the climate emergency'. She describes vividly how she covers protests using her mobile phone, making the most of technology to combine live coverage of multi protests shot on mobiles into one single live stream that is distributed globally, and how she filmed a vicar at one protest who had sewn up his lips because 'climate science and truth has been muted, those who suffer are not being heard'.

Designed to tackle car pollution London's Ultra Low Exclusion Zones (Ulez) have now become a front line in climate journalism among London based journalists. Maggie Brown, a formidable former media editor, has no time whatsoever for LTNs - Low Traffic Networks. Her coruscating piece tells the story of the impact of the zones on the neighbourhood where she lives in Southeast London, Dulwich. She passionately believes 'LTN policy is a lesson in how not to do climate change policy'. In response, a highly respected transport journalist, Christian Wolmar, does not pull his punches. He attacks Maggie Brown's lack of a 'cogent argument' against LTNs to mount a robust defence of the zones. The aim of the introduction of Ulez, LTNs, and 20mph limits is 'to tame the car' so people can enjoy living in their neighbourhoods. They are 'not anti-motorist but pro – people' and he urges Maggie Brown to get on side to campaign for safer healthier urban neighbourhoods.

Accuracy matters

All good journalists do their very best to make sure their reporting is accurate. 'Get it right, get it first' was a mantra at Sky. Accuracy matters in a world full of so much disinformation; it helps to build trust among audiences. It's no accident the licence fee funded broadcaster has recently launched a high-profile campaign 'BBC Verify' to champion the fact that its journalists do check their facts. It's worth remembering there is an organisation to help journalists get their reporting right in the immediate aftermath of extreme weather events. Using weather data and computing models the World Weather Attribution Institute can say if climate change was responsible or not. And they work at speed - unlike many scientists.

Other big news stories matter too

A final few words of caution - a Parthian shot. Editors need to be wary of letting climate stories block out other highly important news stories that our audiences need to know about and to understand: education, health, welfare, the economy. News organisations must make sure their journalism doesn't lead people to think that preventing climate change is the only important priority that needs sorting out in 21st century Britain. Sadly, it is not. There is also the question of cash. Coverage budgets are shallow these days. Thousands of pounds spent on reporting on the ground wildfires on a Greek island means there are far fewer pounds to be spent on sending correspondents to the front line in Ukraine or finding how MPs are funded with in-depth investigations such as the award winning, revelatory 'Westminster Accounts' initiative produced by Sky News and Tortoise Media. Beware, too, the impact of reporting too much doom. Some parts of the world do face being razed but climate journalism must convey a hope that humans can survive. Reports that emphasise only the precarity of imminent disaster can encourage the public to believe it is far too late to take action. Let's be clear in all our journalism: the future is in our hands, at least for the moment.

About the contributor

John Ryley is co-editor of *Toxic News*.

SECTION TWO

Climate change, the debate

Chapter 1

Why has nobody managed to talk about climate change well?

No great speeches or great rhetoric about climate change? **Philip Collins** knows how to write a great speech. He did it for Tony Blair for five years. He asks about the absence of a memorable speech about this existential threat to the planet

There have been some good speeches on climate change down the years. But it is hard to think of one that would count as great. Look through the anthologies of the finest speeches and they rarely, if ever, include a speech that addresses the great existential issue of our time. That seems strange. Maybe it is just a matter of time. Maybe the definitive climate change speech is on the horizon and we will soon find an eloquent leader speaking for the world on the issues which threatens its very survival.

On the face of it, climate change is the perfect candidate for communication in a speech for the ages. It seems to obey all the rules for what makes an enduring item of rhetoric. There is a clear and present danger. We can see the potentially ruinous consequences of inaction or of the wrong course of action. It is something about which people care and on which people are divided. Most political questions are too small to warrant the grand style of the truly epic speech. This is not the case with climate change which could hardly be bigger. So, in a sense, we have it all. The occasion, the issue, and the public attention. Yet somehow the great speech never quite happens.

Some attempts

There have been plenty of very good speeches on what we now call climate change. In a 1963 statement to Congress, the American conservationist and author of the bestseller *Silent Spring* Rachel Carson identified industrial pollution as one of 'the major problems of modern life'. President Richard Nixon dedicated upwards of a third of his 1970 State of the Union address to the environment, describing 'restoring nature to its natural state' as 'a cause beyond party and beyond factions'. It was a reminder that conservation shared more than a phonetic association with conservatism.

The same message was heard in 1989 when the British Prime Minister Margaret Thatcher warned the UN's General Assembly that 'mankind and his activities […] are changing the environment of our planet in dangerous ways'. She demanded a 'realistic programme of action' which was hardly forthcoming at the time. In 2000, at the Kyoto Climate Change Conference, American Vice President Al Gore called on world leaders to 'commit to secure our common destiny: a planet whole and healthy'. Nineteen years later, climate campaigner Greta Thunberg rebuked world leaders gathered at the UN Climate Action

Summit for their subsequent lack of commitment: “We will not let you get away with this”.

Why no great speeches?

These are all speeches of note but none of them quite live at the altitude of the greatest. Is there a reason for that or is it just a quirk of history and the gap will be filled in due course? The phrase-making is not of the highest standard in any of the cases here but that could easily be corrected. Are we just some clever writing away from a great speech? I suspect not. I suspect there are good reasons for supposing that it is more than a quirk and that the absence of a great speech on climate change tells us something fundamental about the act of communicating on the issue.

Lesson from history

To understand what that might it is instructive to look at a speech from a previous era on a subject which was, in its day, the biggest that faced the nation. On 3 April 1872 Benjamin Disraeli, the leader of the Conservative party and leader of the opposition, stood in the Free Trade Hall in Manchester and delivered a speech on public health. It was in part a worrying diagnosis of the susceptibility of the urban population to chronic and contagious diseases and in part a suggestion – rather interestingly for a Conservative politician – that the power of the central state should be galvanised to make improvements. As a speech it hung together well and it included the kind of rhetorical and linguistic flourishes that you might expect from a novelist.

But that's not what made the speech memorable. Lots of speeches are well ordered and some of them are well written too. There are two reasons Disraeli's 1872 speech has lasted. The first is that it named a significant problem. The second is that it proposed a way to deal with it and – this bit is crucial – the man who was speaking genuinely had the power to fix the problem he was identifying.

This is where the great climate change speech goes missing. There is, of course, a significant problem or even a set of significant problems. It is not beyond the wit of a speaker, either, to propose what might be done about them. But that is where it goes awry because those proposals will, by the nature of the problem, be global. The speaker, even if it is the Vice President of the United States, lacks the agency to fix the problem. In the Britain of 1872 Disraeli could promise an infrastructure programme to bring better sanitation to the cities and, as Prime Minister from 1875, that is exactly what his government did. The words took their force from the agency of the speaker. That just doesn't work in the same way for climate change.

One actor is not big enough for this drama

The method of change with this problem is so dispersed, so global, so vast, so out of the hands of any single actor. The act of communication therefore has to be about partnership, bridge-building, and slow progress. Very good, intelligent public speech is, of course, still possible but change is hard. It is often said that the main rhetorical problem with climate change is that speakers have a tendency to inflate the danger and that makes audiences feel like the issue is too large and the cause too hopeless. It is true that the issue is too large but not in that sense. The main communication problem is that nobody is in charge and speeches come alive when the speaker can promise meaningful action. Climate change, sadly, is bigger and harder than any one leader can say.

About the contributor

Philip Collins is an opinion columnist for *The Times*. He was the chief leader writer for the paper for five years. In a previous life he was Prime Minister Tony Blair's Chief Speech Writer for five years, leaving Number 10 on the same day as the former PM and penning his last speech in office.

Chapter 2

Reporting climate: another media failure?

Not all journalists sing from the same hymn sheet on climate change. There are the climate sceptics, critics call them deniers. They range from Charles Moore to Allison Pearson to **Robin Aitken**, former BBC correspondent, who now writes opinion pieces for the *Daily Telegraph*

Let's start from first principles. Any story worth reporting must pass the 'is this important?' test. With climate change the answer has to be 'yes'. Even if you are sceptical of some of the more lurid predictions (I am) any fundamental change in the world's climate affects all humanity so its importance is undeniable. We need to understand as best we can how our climate works and how it is changing so we can prepare and adapt. Climate change is one of a handful of topics that cannot be dismissed as trivial or of sectional interest only. Potentially it affects everyone.

If we accept that the climate is changing (I do) and, therefore, that it is important to try to understand the implications, what obligations flow from that for journalists? The answer is that the first duty of media in a free country is to facilitate the widest possible debate on public policy. Enabling a full-throated debate on climate change is a journalistic duty. There are two reasons for this; firstly, in a democracy it is vitally important that people are well-informed so that when they cast their vote they do so in possession of salient facts; and secondly, a vigorous debate in the public media is the most effective way of guiding policy makers towards wise actions. Wide-ranging debate informs public opinion, which acts on politicians through the ballot box; this is the way modern democracy works.

How has the UK media done on climate change?

Which brings us to the question of the moment: how has our media acquitted itself in the climate change debate? My answer to that is 'very badly'. The UK media's handling of the climate debate is an alarming example of what happens when political polarisation and groupthink infects the very institutions entrusted with providing a public platform for fair and balanced debate. As a result, we have no debate on climate change. Instead what we have is an official position, to which all the major political parties, the scientific establishment, and the heritage media have signed-up. This official narrative, endlessly repeated, tells us that unless we adopt certain (very expensive) policies we are heading for disaster.

They might be right; perhaps the consequences of a warming climate are genuinely catastrophic - that is certainly the line peddled by the BBC and the other mainstream broadcasters (GB News seems less persuaded). But there is an unsettling background flow of contradictory scientific findings. Such material is easy enough to find – it is often covered in non-aligned newspapers like the *Daily Telegraph*, the *Daily Mail*, and *The Times* – but it is almost never picked up by the broadcasters who seem determined that nothing should disturb their doom-laden narrative. Any challenge to the consensus is treated like heresy; the heretics are slandered as 'conspiracy theorists' or, in the cant phrase, as 'climate-deniers'.

Is there a conspiracy on climate change? Who is guilty?

Any time you hear something described as a 'conspiracy theory' or someone as a 'conspiracy theorist' be on your guard: belittling some individual because they believe something different from you is no substitute for engaging with their argument. Those people, serious scientists among them, who think the official climate change narrative overstates the problem and will result in colossal and wasteful state spending deserve a hearing. Instead, what we have ended up with is a media consensus, based on a blind belief in 'the science' which looks more like propaganda than open-minded journalism. The result of this dereliction is a one-sided debate more like an ad campaign than proper journalism. This does real damage: by promoting blind trust in climate models (no model is anything other than a best guess) and giving prominence to the scary future scenarios that flow from them, we have lumbered ourselves with costly policies of unproven efficacy.

British Biased Corporation?

The public broadcasters, BBC and ITV, are supposed to be impartial, and the regulator, OFCOM, is supposed to ensure they are so. It is the broadcasters' decision to silence dissent on climate change which has brought the debate to its present calamitous pass. The BBC, in particular, is blatantly partisan, always ready to amplify the latest scare story relating to climate change. Why is this so? Stories about climate change rose steadily up the agenda throughout the 1990s, and in 2006 the BBC convened a private climate change seminar where senior BBC people were briefed by leading scientific experts and climate activists. The following year the BBC Trust stated: "The BBC has held a high-level seminar with some of the best scientific experts and has come to the view that the weight of evidence no longer justifies equal space being given to the opponents of the consensus."

It is fair, I think, for news reports to assume that climate change is a reality, but the 2007 statement has been interpreted by BBC editors in such a way as to exclude *all* dissent which has resulted in a seriously skewed debate. The BBC matters; despite declining audience share, the Corporation is still the most important media organisation in the country and profoundly shapes public opinion. Because of its perverse interpretation of the 2006 seminar the BBC has thrown all its weight behind supporting expensive policies which might turn out to be predicated on mistaken predictions.

I have not written much about climate change but in the *Daily Telegraph* I once touched on some research findings which are difficult to square with the climate lobby's increasingly apocalyptic predictions: firstly, the frequency of Atlantic hurricanes has shown no increase in the past 150 years; secondly, the number of people worldwide who die from climate-related events has decreased by 60 per cent since the 1970s; and thirdly, there is no evidence that the number of wildfires is increasing; in fact the evidence points the other way. The sources of all of these findings are impeccable: *Nature Communications*; *National Geographic*; and the Royal Society.

I am not qualified to judge this evidence scientifically but it strongly suggests that there is at least a debate to be had about whether things are as calamitous as is being painted. But the BBC never allows these awkward findings to intrude on their preferred narrative of catastrophic climate change. That starting point is then used to bolster the case for policies like net zero.

Why are our media so one sided?

Our media is, theoretically, sceptical, and impartially curious, so why is it exclusively invested in the disaster narrative?

There are two reasons. Firstly, we are schooled by popular culture to over-dramatise reality. A million movie pitches depend upon a McGuffin that boils down to: 'If we don't do this something *really, really bad* will happen'. So, to the newsdesk it's: *'End of the world, uh? Great story. Get on it'*. And off goes our climate change reporter primed to scare us all to death.

The second reason is the new secular religion of scientism which puts scientists and their work on a pedestal. Believers silence dissenters by saying, 'How dare you argue with The Science? It's irrefutable'. But it isn't. Remember the pandemic: those who argued against lockdown policies were silenced by The Science which, we were told, justified lockdown; public dissent was quashed. Looking back, we can see that lockdown was a pointless and damaging exercise which ruined the country's finances whilst doing almost nothing to lower the death rate.

The name of the game

And scientists too have feet of clay. In August 2023 American climate scientist, Patrick Brown, had a paper published in *Nature* arguing that a warming climate has increased the likelihood of wildfires in California. This was dutifully reported by other mainstream media outlets. Then Brown bowled a googly, not only to his readers but also to his co-authors: in an online article, blog post, and social media posts he said he had deliberately downplayed or suppressed contradictory evidence in order to achieve publication. He alleged that other scientists do this too because, unless they stick to the disaster script, they won't get funding for their research teams. Scientists are fallible and sometimes venal; as well as searching for scientific truth they also care about their careers and incomes.

There is far too little scepticism in the British media about climate change. The BBC, and other broadcasters, predictably now link every wildfire, every drought, every heavy rain storm to climate change. The Corporation is like the bloke in the High Street with 'The End is Nigh' billboard strapped to his back. On the strength of its doomsday predictions we are being encouraged to adopt expensive and unproven technologies like electric vehicles and heat pumps. There are counter-facts: owning a conventional car, maintaining it well and running it into the ground is the most eco-friendly way of motoring. In this way you can get 200,000 miles from a conventional model (I have done this several times). EVs, Electric Vehicles, by contrast, rely on batteries that cannot be replaced and have a limited lifespan; this is highly wasteful of scarce and valuable resources.

I do not know if the climate change doom-mongers are right or wrong but I do know when I am the victim of media groupthink; the general public can sense this too. The Brexit vote in 2016 came as a great shock to our political and media elites because voters rejected their fanatical Europhilia. So far voters have had only limited opportunities to have their say on climate change policies; our elites may be in for a nasty shock if they ever do. Journalists, let the sunlight in! There is nothing to fear from open debate; it is the best way of establishing truth.

References

John Bridcut (Junc 2007) 'From seesaw to wagon wheel – a report into impartiality in the 21st century', London, BBC Trust.

Patrick Brown, Steven J Davis, and Craig Clements (2023) 'Climate warming increases extreme daily wildfire growth risk in California', *Nature* DOI/s41586-023-06444-3

The Royal Society (2020) 'Global trends in wildfire and its impacts', 2 October.

Madeleine Stone (2021) 'Weather-related deaths are down – warming could undo that trend', *National Geographic*, 11 October.

Gabriel A Vecchi, Christopher Ophel Landsea, Wei Zhang, Gabriele Villarini, and Thomas Knutson (2021) 'Changes in Atlantic major hurricane frequency since the late-19th century', *Nature Communications,* 12, 4054

About the contributor

Robin Aitken is a former BBC news correspondent on *Today*, *The World Tonight*, and *Breakfast News*. He now writes columns for *The Daily Telegraph* mainly on media matters.

Chapter 3

After Brexit comes the great net zero betrayal

Rishi Sunak is applying the same populist playbook that took us out of the EU to climate change policy. This time, argues **Matthew d'Ancona**, the stakes are existential

When you have done all you can to wreck the nation, what do you do next? Answer: move on to wrecking the planet. It should really be no surprise that the gang that brought us Brexit has now turned its attention to sabotaging the UK's chances of meeting its net zero target by 2050. Politically, psychologically and strategically, the two projects are intimately connected; they are two sides of the same ugly coin.

Since the Conservatives unexpectedly held on to Uxbridge and South Ruislip in July 2023 - albeit by the slender margin of 495 votes - Rishi Sunak has made quite clear that his enthusiasm for green policies is distinctly limited. Mindful of the role that opposition to Mayor Sadiq Khan's extension of London's Ultra Low Emission Zone (Ulez) played in the by-election, he told the *Sunday Telegraph* that, "I just want to make sure people know that I'm on their side in supporting them to use their cars to do all the things that matter to them"; unveiled a review of low traffic neighbourhoods (LTNs); and denounced Labour as 'anti-motorist'.

Eleven days after the by-election, the PM announced a 'maxing out' policy in the North Sea and 100-plus new drilling licences. Though HMG remains notionally committed to net zero, he declared then that the target set by the 2015 Paris agreement should not 'unnecessarily give people more hassle and more costs in their lives'.

In September, he went even further in an extraordinary speech, notable principally for its brazen moral complacency. As he postponed a series of crucial deadlines – in particular, the year after which new cars will have to be electric – he claimed that the UK's net zero strategy was so far ahead in international rankings that it could afford to be 'more pragmatic, proportionate, and realistic'.

For the record: the independent Climate Change Committee, which monitors progress on emissions targets, does not share Sunak's confidence. In June, its chairman, Lord Deben, warned that this country had 'lost its clear global climate leadership', was falling behind the US and the European Union, and should remember that 'delay is not an option'.

Is the UK in the van?

Pressed on his new strategy on the *Today* programme, the PM tetchily told Nick Robinson that it was for his critics to "explain to the country why they think it's right that ordinary families up and down the country should have to fork out five, 10, 15 thousand pounds to make the transition earlier than is necessary". This is the diametric opposite of leadership.

But let us say, just for the sake of argument, that the UK *is* indeed ahead of counterpart nations in addressing the climate crisis. In the face of an existential threat, what Sunak calls 'over-delivery' should be the cause of pride, not irritation. Does a fire crew that begins to get on top of a blaze down its hoses and head off for a relaxing lunch?

Climate change policy ought to be governed by a moonshot mentality: the faster the better. Instead, the PM speaks with resentment of the comparative performance of other countries and proposes to slow down British measures accordingly. Ecological disaster is, in the famous framing of the great American psychiatrist Robert Jay Lifton, the 'apocalyptic twin' of nuclear war. Yet Sunak refers to net zero as if it were merely one public policy among many - and by no means the most important. So much for the 'world-leading' UK; so much for 'Global Britain'. This is geopolitics reduced to: After you, Claude!

To put the speech in perspective: it was condemned in the following weekend's *Observer* by the Conservative MP Chris Skidmore as 'the worst kind of culture war politics'. Skidmore is a former minister for energy and clean growth and chaired the government's independent review of net zero. But he was also one of the five authors of the notorious *Britannia Unchained* pamphlet published in 2012 (the other four were Priti Patel, Kwasi Kwarteng, Dominic Raab, and Liz Truss); hardly an 'eco-zealot', then. (By way of contrast, Donald Trump congratulated Sunak for 'recognising this SCAM before it was too late'.)

For Brexit read Clexit?

What lies behind all this? Just as he backed Brexit in 2016 on predominantly economic grounds, claiming that the UK's departure from the EU would liberate British business from Brussels bureaucracy, so Sunak is instinctively suspicious of green commitments as yet another regulatory imposition upon the free market by the state. In this, he is following the example of his role model and predecessor as chancellor, the late Nigel Lawson, who was chair of the Vote Leave campaign and of the Global Warming Policy Foundation that opposes what Lawson called 'the new religion of eco-fundamentalism'.

Not all Brexiteers, it is true, are climate sceptics: in June 2023, Zac Goldsmith resigned from the government in protest at its 'apathy in the face of the greatest challenge we have faced' and the extent to which 'this existential challenge leaves you [Sunak] personally unmoved'. To drive home the point, the Conservative peer said that he could be 'very tempted' to back Labour on climate policy.

In general, however, those Tories who pursued Brexit most vigorously are also those now challenging net zero measures. There is a striking membership overlap between the longstanding parliamentary European Research Group and the newer Net Zero Scrutiny Group, chaired by Craig Mackinlay MP and co-founded by his fellow pro-Brexit 'Spartan' Steve Baker.

In July, Lord Frost, the former chief Brexit negotiator, claimed, extraordinarily, that rising global temperatures are 'likely to be beneficial' to the UK. Though an insult to the public's intelligence, his remark also demonstrated the cultural affinity for this cohort of Conservatives between Brexitism and climate scepticism.

Both ideologies involve a shocking indifference to evidence and data. They reflect a bulldog belief that Britain will always be better off pursuing its own path, rather than engaging with supranational negotiations and institutions. They share a distaste for 'experts' - economists in the case of Brexit, the world's scientists in the case of climate change. In many instances, Brexiteers and eco-sceptics express the same paranoid suspicion of 'global elites' and 'globalist conspiracies'.

We are all in favour of net zero. Are we?

Note that almost nobody expresses open hostility to the core project of emissions reduction and the achievement of net zero – at some point. At present, the argument is about the pace and cost to the public of the measures that are necessary if the UK is to stand a chance of meeting its commitments.

Remember: Brexit did not start with outright demands for the UK to leave the EU but a steady chipping away of public confidence in Brussels and its treatment of

Britain. A similarly incremental strategy is being adopted to kill off net zero: step by step, stage by stage. And once again, Nigel Farage is the key figure, moving further and faster than most Conservative MPs are prepared to go for now. In March 2022, he launched his new anti-net zero campaign, Britain Means Business, arguing that "by taking Britain down its ruinous path, the political class in Westminster has made a decision on behalf of the rest of us without any public debate being held [...] The same high-minded principles that pertained to Britain's membership of the EU apply to net zero". Farage is demanding a referendum on the emissions target, and some polls suggest that the public – though still broadly supportive of net zero – is attracted by the idea of another such public vote. It is all horribly familiar.

At this point, the objective is to undermine the public and political consensus on climate change, to sow the seeds of doubt and to create political division. This is the classic disruptive playbook, first devised by the tobacco industry and now the basis of most populist politics. And, already, it has put the frighteners on Sir Keir Starmer, who panicked in the wake of the Uxbridge by-election and has significantly toned-down Labour's commitment to environmental measures.

For those who want to thwart the UK's climate commitments, these are gratifying times. With this barely concealed retreat from net zero (Sunak insists, mysteriously, that the target will still be met by 2050) and his claim that 'we risk losing the consent of the British people', the PM has blown a sharp dog whistle to those demanding another referendum. Sunak's message to this hardcore audience is: you won't get such a vote from me – but I'm on your side.

Not the side of the future, though. No Tory leader in modern times has so brazenly rejected Edmund Burke's principle that society is 'a partnership not only between those who are living, but between those who are living, those who are dead, and those who are to be born'.
But Sunak's cohort of Conservative has severed all ties with such traditions. Gone are the days of One Nation Toryism, of centre-right internationalism, of the old conservationist impulse that dwelt in the party's soul. You might think that Brexit would be more than enough for any political generation. It turns out only to be the start.

A version of this chapter first appeared in *The New European.*

About the contributor

Matthew d'Ancona is Editor at Large at *The New European*, where he writes a weekly column and co-hosts The Two Matts podcast with the newspaper's founder Matt Kelly. He is also a Contributing Editor at *Prospect*, and a columnist at the London *Evening Standard*. He is a former editor of *The Spectator*, and deputy editor of *The Sunday Telegraph*. His most recent book is *Ideology, Ignorance, Innovation: Why the Old Politics is Useless & What to Do About It* (Hodder 2021). He posts on X: @MatthewdAncona

Chapter 4

Boris v Rishi, the sequel

Watching Rishi Sunak deliver his controversial climate change U-turn speech, arch Boris Johnson critic **Paul Connew** found himself with an unexpected soft spot for the ex-Prime Minister. He looks at the political intrigue and machinations that led to the U-turn

"Boris, Boris, wherefore art thou, Boris?" I'm not in the habit of delivering paeans to our fallen prime minister. But it sprang to mind on Wednesday 20 September 2023 as I watched the man who ousted him morph into Boris as he staged a speech and press conference at No 10, bluffing and blustering through a transparent retreat on the government's climate change policy. Except that Rishi Sunak lacked the Bojo persona's entertainment quality: no jokes, no Shakespeare quotations, no diversions into Latin, no references to Plato or Socrates or obscure emperor-generals with names plucked from antiquity.

Sunak's seven deadly bins

What was familiar, however, was the cynical opportunism, the liberty with facts, the bogus spin that came with claiming to have scrapped measures that were not even his government's climate change policy agenda, such as taxes on meat, flying, compulsory car-sharing, and forcing households to recycle in seven different bins. Even at his most fanciful Johnson might have shied away from Sunak's claim that his decision 'wasn't political' when that was transparently exactly what it was.

But what was also clear was that 20 September signalled the starting gun for a general election next autumn, or even a snap election gamble next spring, in which climate change retreat will be at the heart of Sunak's bid to turn the electoral tide in a triple-issue harness with migration, and accusations that Keir Starmer is plotting to betray Brexit and steer by stealth Britain back into the EU.

No time for climate change recidivism

It wasn't surprising when Boris Johnson became the first senior Conservative politician to wade in criticising Sunak, warning his successor that he 'cannot afford to falter now and lose our ambition for the country'. I was disappointed he didn't dramatically leap in front of the TV cameras to do it, but a staunch climate change believer member of Clan Johnson tells me, "That was only the start, Boris won't let Rishi off the hook on climate change recidivism over the coming months, regardless of it being a general election year."

That said, it's worth remembering that, as prime minister, Boris Johnson preached a green gospel while also sanctioning a new fossil fuel round of licensing for North Sea oil and gas fields, and backing the plan for a giant new coal mine in Cumbria. The late September licensing go-ahead by regulators for one of them, the huge Rosebank field off the Shetlands, sparked a furious row between environmental groups and the government with campaigners and scientists now planning a legal challenge to try and block it. It increased doubts about Sunak's insistence that Britain will still fulfil its legal obligation to reach net zero by 2050. There was also a cool reception from the government's own advisory body, the Climate Change Committee. Previously it had advocated sticking with Johnson's policy.

The Great Rosebank challenge

The Rosebank decision angered some green Tory MPs but delighted climate change sceptics and downright deniers on the party's right. It also fed into the view of those suspecting Johnson's criticism of Sunak during an election campaign will be oiled as much by personal hostility toward the man he blames for ousting him as PM as his concern for the planet.

Ironically, Johnson's opposition to Sunak's climate change U-turn has united support for him from some of the Tory MPs who were instrumental in his prime ministerial downfall.

Rishi zapped by Zac

Unsurprisingly Johnson's friend and ally Lord Zac Goldsmith, who had earlier quit as a minister citing Rishi Sunak's 'apathy' toward climate change, telling BBC *Newsnight* the prime minister should hold an immediate general election over his 'green policy U-turn'.

Another former cabinet minister Alok Sharma, the man who chaired the COP26 summit in Glasgow, challenged Sunak in an interview with *The Observer* to show how the UK could meet its green pledges in the wake of his backtracking. Ironically, Sharma was at a UN climate change conference in New York attended by a number of international leaders, including US president Joe Biden. Rishi Sunak had been invited but declined and effectively delivered his controversial retreat speech at No10 instead. Sharma's friends suggest his subsequent decision not to stand at the general election reflected his dismay.

Sunak's decision to announce his controversial climate change watering down just ahead of a tricky Conservative party conference and an even trickier, testier COP summit in Dubai, was variously hailed as 'bold' by his supporters and 'folly' by his critics within the Tory ranks as well as from opposition parties.

A dramatic twist was added when billionaire telecoms tycoon John Caudwell, for some time the Tories' biggest individual donor, announced he was so disgusted by Sunak's action he was dropping his support and, in common with Zac Goldsmith, planned to vote Labour unless the prime minister backs down.

Putting the skids under Rishi

Former Tory energy minister Chris Skidmore, the party's leading climate change expert in parliament, went further by saying he would consider mounting a No Confidence bid in the prime minister. It even divided Boris Johnson's most loyal devotees with

Jacob Rees-Mogg, not always complimentary about the present premier, hailing Sunak's action with the politician turned eponymous GB News host, predicting, 'This could win us the general election' and throwing in 'environmentalism must never be allowed to make people poorer'.

By contrast Nadine Dorries, his former Cabinet colleague and rival for the title of Bojo's number one fan girl, struck a different note. The frustrated House of Lords wannabe, now doubling as host of her own show on TalkTV, is sticking to her view that 'global warming is the biggest crisis facing our planet'.

Blue on blue on green

The *Daily Mail* felt obliged to run a 21 September modest sized page lead on the Sunak/Johnson climate change divergence under the headline 'Now it's blue on blue on green' with the capped up red strap 'COMMON SENSE ON NET ZERO' making it plain elsewhere in the edition who it thinks is making sense - and it's not its usual political hero and star columnist Boris. The *Mail* is also constantly on the alert over what it fears might just be a big revolt in parliament drummed up by what it terms 'Tory Wets' to beat Sunak into reversing his own U-turn. The paper blamed the advance leaks of Sunak's plans to the BBC and *The Times* on The Blob, its derogatory term for the civil service they no longer bother to accord scare quotes, even suggesting an alliance with left-wing eco-zealots (again, without scare quotes).

So what lies behind the emerging Sunak strategy of linking climate change costs with the migrant boat crisis and the hotly-disputed accusation Keir Starmer is plotting to take the UK closer to the EU, even eventually reversing Brexit? The migrant boat tactic deliberately ignores the reality that illegal migration is the Siamese twin of climate change for those fleeing fire, flood, and famine, the former two f-words hitting Europe on an unprecedented scale this summer. But it will do nothing to stem the human tide determined to seek 'salvation' in Europe and the UK. It's the reality check neither Sunak nor Starmer really want to confront.

In the short, election-obsessed, term Rishi Sunak, the cool technocrat, is being rebranded as Rishi, the fiery political fighter. It's a desperate plan, a big gamble, but one largely devised by Isaac Levido, the Australian strategy guru and protégé of veteran Tory campaign eminence grise, Sir Lynton 'Wizard of Oz' Crosby.

Levido is largely credited with masterminding Boris Johnson's 2019 general election victory but is now working on undermining and overhauling some of Johnson's policies, not least those on climate change. That move was heavily influenced by the Tories narrowly clinging on to Johnson's own former Uxbridge constituency thanks to hostility to London Mayor Sadiq Khan's Ulez extension edict, despite that being more a public health issue than a climate change one.

Levido the weaponiser

For Levido, however, it represented the elusive political opportunity to devise - in campaign jargon - a wedge issue, a clear dividing line between the Conservatives and Labour, projecting climate change as the opinion poll game changer and election tide-turner that would appeal in crucial Red Wall areas. As Team Levido has it: uber-rich Rishi is cast as the leader 'saving hard-pressed families from unacceptable costs of green policies and Labour as the party piling them on'. One member of that team was overheard in Westminster pub The Red Lion a couple of hours after Sunak's speech declaring, 'Climate change and migration: the combination to bolster our backbenchers who think the only thing Starmer has to do to win is keep saying "Time for a Change".'

In effect, the Sunak/Levido axis had placed a cynical or desperate bid to win votes above the relative cross-party consensus on climate change that had existed in Britain since Thatcher (an early political environmentalist) through Major, Blair, Cameron, May and, yes, Johnson, but not Truss and now Sunak. It was a move that came with private research revealing that cancel culture and anti-woke tactics about issues like gender self-identification or white privilege weren't scoring the way the party's right-wing had bargained for.

Levido, who has also served as a US campaign adviser for the GOP, is a compulsive poll student who champions weaponising the UK right-wing press, and its online audience, over climate change. The theory is that, despite declining print sales, it could yet tilt the general election balance. The idea of an interlinked three-pronged strategy linking climate change, migration, and Brexit betrayal being embraced by both right-wing print titles and new TV disruptors like GB News and TalkTV, is very much the Levido playbook.

Weaponising U-turns

The Levido playbook was clearly in evidence in Sunak's party conference opening day appearance on Laura Kuenssberg's programme in which he variously tried to promote himself as the motorists' champion and the rich man whose climate change retreats showed him more in tune with 'ordinary families' than his political and scientific critics. He also disputed that the shifts jeopardise the legal 2050 net zero commitment. Inconveniently that morning, his Business Secretary Kemi Badenoch told the *Sunday Times* she would favour ditching the 2050 date further into the future.

The Levido strategy certainly affected both the Conservative and Labour Party conferences.

The Tory one saw ministers and right-wing MPs aggressively targeting the high profile Ecotricity clean energy tycoon Dale Vince for being both a major Labour donor (£1.5m) and a major bankroller of Just Stop Oil (£340k plus). But Vince hit back in a *Guardian* op-ed column coinciding with the opening of Labour's conference by announcing he was halting funding Just Stop Oil and urged the group to drop disruptive protests that could be 'counter-productive' to Labour's election prospects. But Levido team members branded Vince's own U-term a 'political gimmick' and vowed to continue targeting him and alleged Labour links to other 'eco zealots' as a key plank of the Tory election strategy.

How the papers responded to Rishi the Switch

'Sunak spares public Net Zero pain' declared the *Telegraph* front page. This was echoed by the *Mail*'s 'I'll spare families ruinous cost of net zero, vows Rishi', with a secondary headline reading 'PM takes on eco zealots in bold move that could transform Tory fortunes'. Inside, the *Mail* unleashed favoured polemicist Stephen Glover under a huge headline 'He's under attack from Labour, the BBC and the Blob, but this is by far the most daring Rishi's done as PM!'.

The *Daily Express* settled for 'Honest Rishi: Nation Won't And Can't Pay Net Zero Bill'. Curiously, the *Express*'s Labour-backing Reach stablemate, *The Mirror*, was alone in not featuring Sunak's speech on its front page the morning after. There are whispers the normally pro-green title was spooked by earlier reader feedback heavily hostile to Mayor Khan's Ulez expansion plan with some welcoming Labour's failure to capture Uxbridge.

For its part, *The Times* went for a matter of fact 'Sunak's green targets gamble' and, to its credit, has largely followed through with leaders, columnists and scientists reflecting both sides of the debate. Its tabloid stablemate *The Sun* went for the short and snappy: 'GIVEN US A BRAKE!'

Opportunity knocks for the Lib Dems?

Andrew Rawnsley, chief political columnist at *The Observer*, speculated that Sunak's gamble could backfire by boosting the election chances of the Lib Dems in Tory-held targets seats in the South and West Country where climate change sympathies run high. Rawnsley argued powerfully, 'In a single statement lasting less than an hour, the Tory leader stuffed many of his party's previous commitments into the waste bin disposal, enraged environmental campaigners, aggravated carmakers, the renewable energy industry and the financial sector; and split his party'.

With climate change to the fore and migrant boats moored alongside and Brexit not yet dead in the water, we are firmly on course for a very bitter, explosive, divisive general election with the future of the planet at stake.

About the contributor

Paul Connew is a media commentator, broadcaster, ex-editor of the *Sunday Mirror*, deputy editor of the *Daily Mirror*, former Mirror Group US bureau chief, and (pre-phone hacking) deputy editor of the *News of the World*. A regular judge of the British Press Awards, he writes and broadcasts on media and politics for a number of organisations including the BBC, Sky News, CNN, GB News, LBC, Talk TV, Australian Broadcasting, Al-Jazeera, *The New European*, Netflix, Amazon, and The Drum website.

Chapter 5

Climate change news values are evolving

UK media's climate coverage changed dramatically this century. **Malcolm Bradbrook** examines the growing recognition that it affects all areas of society

Until very recently, 'climate fatigue' was highlighted by journalism editors as a reason not to cover issues around sustainability and climate change.

The 'classic' specialisms such as crime, health, and education were often seen on front pages or leading bulletins in the United Kingdom. Coverage of environmental issues was kept to major international events such as the UN annual Conference of Parties (COP), extreme events such as flooding or heatwaves, and new species of fauna being seen in this country.

News values at the start of this century can be classified as below:

1. The power elite: Stories concerning powerful individuals, organisations or institutions.
2. Celebrity: Stories concerning people who are already famous.
3. Entertainment: Stories concerning sex, showbusiness, human interest, animals, an unfolding drama, or offering opportunities for humorous treatment, entertaining photographs or witty headlines.

4. Surprise: Stories that have an element of surprise and/or contrast.
5. Bad news: Stories with particularly negative overtones, such as conflict or tragedy.
6. Good news: Stories with particularly positive overtones, such as rescues and cures.
7. Magnitude: Stories that are perceived as sufficiently significant either in the numbers of people involved or in potential impact.
8. Relevance: Stories about issues, groups, and nations perceived to be relevant to the audience.
9. Follow-up: Stories about subjects already in the news.

(Harcup and O'Neill 2001, 278–279)

Surprising and bizarre

As a freelance journalist ten years ago, my experience was that it was very difficult to get a climate or sustainability story commissioned in news outlets unless it was under 'surprise', and specifically, surprising stories that had an element of 'the bizarre'.

One story I had commissioned by the *International Business Times* was around the most sustainable treatment of a dead body. With the headline 'Is death the final green frontier? The Corpse Project investigates the sustainability of dying', the article ticked the right 'bizarre' boxes, but my pitches around impact of climate change on soil erosion or water quality could not live up to this catchy precedent.

International Business Times

Science | Environment

Is death the final green frontier? The Corpse Project investigates the sustainability of dying

Report calls for better understanding of the environmental impact of death, challenging burial myths.

IBT VIDEO

Kangaroo fight caught on police infrared camera

(Screenshot taken in 2017. Content now archived by *The International Business Times*)

I wrote several articles around tackling climate change for lifestyle magazines that focused on fitness. These generally were tips-based features, based upon what runners or cyclists or swimmers or triathletes could do to minimise the impact they had on the environment, but the big successes only came when, again, I tapped into 'the bizarre'.

In 2017 I wrote an article for *Runner's World* magazine which profiled Rima Chang, an ultra-runner who competed at events dragging a tyre behind her to raise awareness of the need to reduce our use of disposable plastic. With a headline of 'Why this runner completes marathons dragging a tyre behind her', it was irresistible to the commissioning editor and to runners Googling the term 'marathon' (*Runner's World,* 2017).

Campaigning organisations struggled to secure the coverage they desired to raise awareness of specific environmental issues by traditional means such as a press release or event. I created all of the content (about 14,000 words spread across six features) on one large 'sponsored content' project for *The Daily Telegraph.* The Woodland Trust felt it had no choice but to pay high prices for such an 'owned-content' project on the subject of tree disease despite the issue being a major threat to flora and worsening with climate change.

An end to 'change' and 'sceptics'

However, change has been noticed across the media in the past decade.

In 2019, *The Guardian* announced that its language about environmentalism was evolving with the traditional 'climate change' being replaced by 'climate crisis', and 'climate denier' being preferred to 'climate sceptic' (*The Guardian*, 2019). Two years later, Fiona Harvey, the environment correspondent of *The Guardian*, noted that, "The job of environment correspondent still involves warnings about the future, but climate breakdown and the crisis in nature can no longer be regarded as 'slow burn' – they are emergencies happening now and must be treated as such" (*The Guardian,* 2021).

Leaving the vertical for the horizontal in the news values reckoning

In the past five years much seems to have changed and with it has come a recognition that climate crisis reporting has become more 'mainstream' across the media. This seems to be an acceptance that a change to news values has been needed when dealing with such a large and far-reaching subject.

There is a greater understanding that the climate crisis affects many areas and so it has evolved from a vertical topic to a horizontal topic (see Fig1).

News Values: The Vertical & The Horizontal

		Vertical topics						
		Health	Education	Sport	Business	Travel	Music	Fashion
Horizontal Topics	-Politics -Finance -Environment	Hospital waiting lists	Attainment in schools	Olympics	Changing high street	Rising fuel costs	Stadium gigs	Fast fashion
		Childhood diseases	Exams and changing trends	Super League	Post Brexit implications	Red list countries	New releases	The rise of thrifting
		GP recruitment etc.	Gender bias	NUFC takeover	Jobs creation	Water quality	Merch	Supermodels

Fig 1 (source: Malcolm Bradbrook)

The vertical topics are those traditional specialisms employed by the national media in the United Kingdom. The environment has also existed as a specialism on some platforms, most notably the *BBC, The Guardian*, and Channel 4 but was not present in all newsrooms.

Horizontal topics are those which reach across all vertical topics as well as having specific stories coming under them. A political editor would cover general elections, party conferences, political promotions etc., but the implications of decisions made by politicians would be felt across many sectors: funding for hospitals in manifesto announcements, setting targets for schools, bidding for the Olympics, the Chancellor's latest pledge on rising fuel costs, noise pollution policy and its impact on stadium gigs, and potential changes to taxation on second-hand clothing stores.

In recent years it seems as though the environment and the climate crisis has been added to the list of horizontal subjects.

Stories about hospital waiting lists may be influenced by the climate crisis as excess deaths increase during harsher winters and hotter summers. Some state schools struggle to provide temperature-controlled exams rooms capable of managing extreme summers such as those in 2022. Fast fashion and the drive for low-cost production are most likely to affect those developing countries most susceptible to climate change.

The impact on the natural world around us has been gradually included in all topics. This has widened discussion.

Even the *Daily Mail* changes tack

Examples in the news that have already been included come from *The Guardian*, which has a long tradition of supporting climate change/climate crisis journalism. However, this change has been noted across the sector, although the quantity of articles varies between platforms.

The *Daily Mail* has shown examples of adopting this new approach to environmental coverage as a horizontal subject. Headlines such as 'How climate change could affect when and where you travel (with GREENLAND set to cash in on tourists escaping blowtorch summer temperatures)' show this new direction (*MailOnline*, 2023).

Other publishing brands have produced articles related to fashion. The *Financial Times* has incorporated this approach with headlines such as 'Why fast fashion is still not available in green' (*Financial Times,* 2023). Reuters produced a deep dive into levels of waste in the fashion industry with the headline 'Resale is all the rage, but fashion brands not making a dent in unsustainable levels of waste' (Reuters, 2023).

The way forward

But there is still huge work to be done for journalists covering this area.

Journalism researcher Craig Robertson states, "The story can seem intractable, depressing, and often difficult to understand. It is also frequently politicised, with audiences polarised on the topic" (Reuters Institute, 2022a). He highlights the fact that those audiences most receptive to climate crisis stories are those who have had first-hand exposure to the extreme challenges it can bring. He adds, "Many countries have witnessed extreme weather events linked to climate change; Greece and Portugal, for instance, have suffered from devastating wildfires in recent years, and Chile continues to suffer from severe drought, which has made climate change 'easy to see'. It may be that audiences are more interested in news about the topic when they are not so polarised and can clearly see the negative effects of extreme weather where they live" (Reuters Institute, 2022b).

References

Malcolm Bradbrook (2017) 'Why this runner completes marathons dragging a tyre behind her', Available at https://www.runnersworld.com/uk/training/motivation/a775712/why-this-runner-completes-marathons-dragging-a-tyre-behind-her/ (Accessed: 26 September 2023).

Amy Brown (2023) 'Resale is all the rage, but fashion brands not making a dent in unsustainable levels of waste' Available at: https://www.reuters.com/sustainability/climate-energy/resale-is-all-rage-fashion-brands-not-making-dent-unsustainable-levels-waste-2023-08-09/ (Accessed: 26 September 2023)

Tony Harcup and Deirdre O'Neill (2001) 'What is News? Galtung and Ruge Revisited', *Journalism Studies* 2 (2): 261–280. doi: 10.1080/14616700118449 [Taylor & Francis Online]

Fiona Harvey (2021) 'Reporting on the climate crisis: "For years it was seen as a far-off problem"', *The Guardian*, 26 August.

Craig T Roberston (2022) 'How people access and think about climate change news' Available at: https://reutersinstitute.politics.ox.ac.uk/digital-news-report/2022/how-people-access-and-think-about-climate-change-news (Accessed: 27 September 2023).

Alice Ross (2023) 'Why fast fashion is still not available in green' Available at: https://www.ft.com/content/8fed1e01-f685-4752-adc5-422b06493eee (Accessed: 26 September 2023).

Laura Sharman (2023) 'How climate change could affect when and where you travel (with GREENLAND set to cash in on tourists escaping blowtorch summer temperatures)' Available at: https://www.dailymail.co.uk/travel/article-12561757/How-climate-change-affect-people-travel.html (Accessed: 26 September 2023).

Sophie Zeldon-O'Neill (2019) *'It's a crisis, not a change': the six Guardian language changes on climate matters'* Available at: https://www.theguardian.com/environment/2019/oct/16/guardian-language-changes-climate-environment? (Accessed: 26 September 2023).

About the contributor

Malcolm Bradbrook has been a journalist for 26 years and written on sustainability for UK regional media, *The Daily Telegraph*, the *International Business Times*, and magazines such as *Outdoor Fitness*, *Runner's World*, and *Tri220*. He worked for four years as a Senior Communications Manager with Earthwatch, an environmental research and education NGO.

Chapter 6

Climate change: a deep dive into 20 years of Google search trends

Whatever people say in response to opinion pollsters, more is often revealed about the public's attitudes by their online search history. **Isabelle Marchand** examines the data

Amid the cost-of-living crisis, Prime Minister Rishi Sunak made a pivotal move by scaling back green initiatives, wagering that when purse strings tighten, climate change aspirations take a back seat. Though Google Trends and historical data initially seemed to back this theory, a closer look reveals more intricate patterns. While the financial crisis 15 years ago prompted a shift in priorities, today's landscape paints a different picture. People might care less about major climate change news, but local initiatives still raise interest.

Unsurprisingly, financial hardship dampens interest in climate change

This chart shows how major economic events can affect public discourse and interest. Notably, we observed a significant dip in searches related to climate change in the aftermath of the 2007-08 financial crisis. This decline likely mirrors the public's shifting priorities during times of economic strain: immediate financial concerns can overshadow longer-term, albeit equally pressing, issues like climate change.

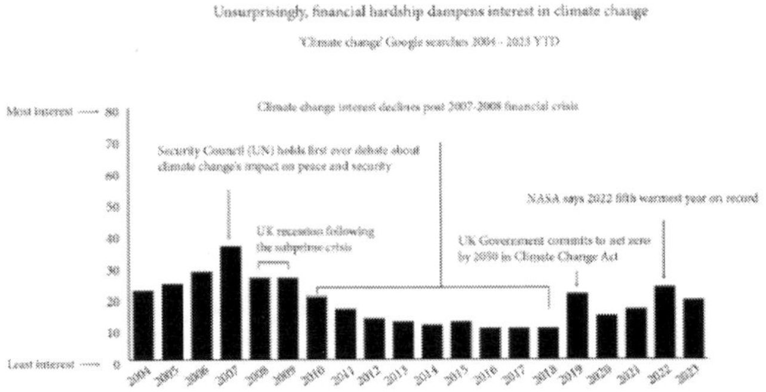

Fast forward to 2023, and we're witnessing a similar scenario play out. The UK is grappling with a severe cost-of-living crisis, which understandably dominates public attention. Given this backdrop, Prime Minister Rishi Sunak's recent softening of the UK's green stance might be aimed at providing short-term relief to a population grappling with economic hardships, with an eye on the looming 2025 general elections.

Public interest in climate change frequently correlates with increased local initiatives and legislation

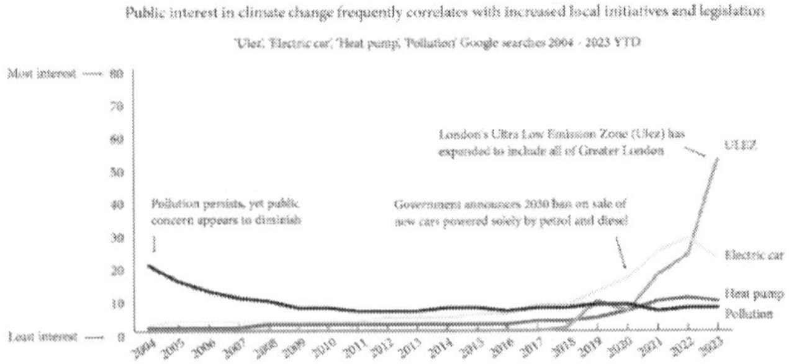

Ecological concerns evolve over time. In the 2000s, ‘pollution’ was Googled more than it is today. Yet, with stringent emission controls imposed on industries, transport, and homes in recent years, air quality has notably improved, making it cleaner than it's been since the Industrial Revolution. This progress might account for the reduced searches for pollution: the issue is on the mend.

In 2023, topics such as the expansion of Ulez across Greater London are making headlines. This scheme imposes a £12.50 daily charge on older, high-emission vehicles traversing the zone. Simultaneously, heat pumps have gained traction due to government grants promoting their adoption. Similarly, a blend of technological advancements, governmental backing, and heightened ecological consciousness has amplified interest in electric cars since 2018. Climate change is multidimensional with its intricate ripple effects touching our everyday lives. While the broad concept of climate change may seem elusive to some, the past 15 years of media coverage and strategic measures have cultivated a more ecologically conscious mindset than we saw a decade and a half ago.

Although flooding is still a major concern in the UK, ‘heatwave’ Google searches are on the rise

While 'flood' remains a dominant search term in the UK, there's a notable uptick in searches for 'heatwave'. This shift can be attributed to recent climate patterns, as several of the past years have been marked as the hottest on record by NASA. As extreme temperatures become more commonplace due to global warming, the British public's search behaviour mirrors this growing concern, highlighting the changing face of climate-related challenges in the UK.

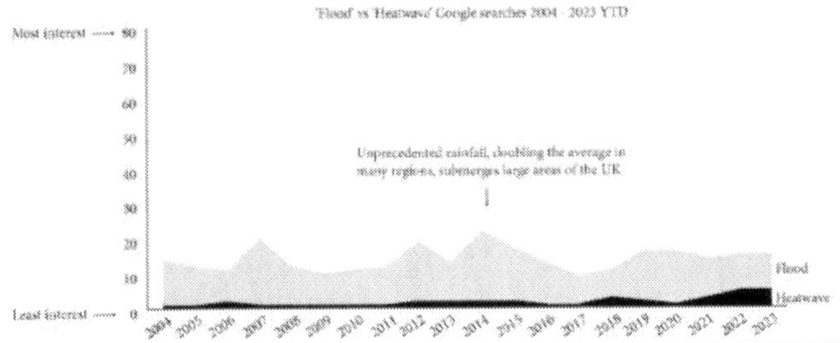

Interest in 'net zero' has been rising since 2018

Net zero by 2050 means that the UK aims to remove as many greenhouse gases from the atmosphere as it emits. To achieve this, businesses and industries across all sectors must work towards drastically reducing their emissions.

The idea of net zero really started to catch on globally around the 2015 Paris Agreement. However, as the chart below shows, public interest began to rise notably three years later, in 2018. It is now at an all-time high.

While political moves often echo public sentiment, Rishi Sunak's rollback on net zero is a gamble. Although a *Times* newspaper poll suggests that 76 per cent of Conservative voters supported the decision, broader perspectives from Labour (16 per cent support), not to mention typically green-supportive

Green and Lib Dem voters, show less enthusiasm. As climate challenges increasingly affect daily life, today's voters are more aware of the need for green policies than they were 15 years ago and, as a consequence, Sunak's bet might not yield the returns he anticipated.

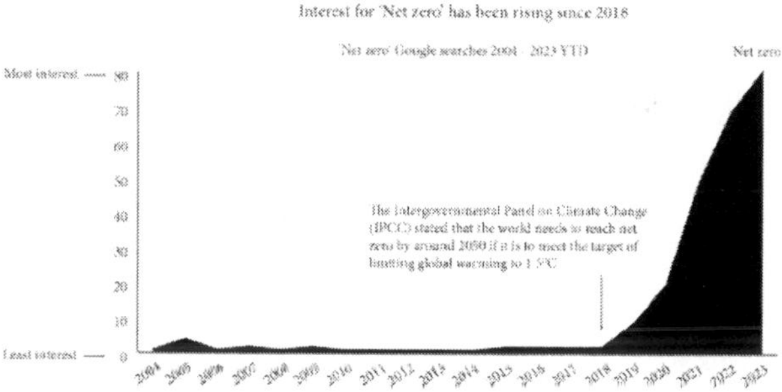

References

Damian Carrington and Steven Morris (2014) 'Flood simple: the UK flooding crisis explained', *The Guardian*, 13 February.

Greenpeace (2019) 'What is 'net zero', and how can we get there?' Available at: https://www.greenpeace.org.uk/news/net-zero/?gclid=CjwKCAjwgsqoBhBNEiwAwe5w07DWFmP9wiftRICnJLtjOcwUkH-gufuU_pezMEqDo04aOUpcd2CoERoCV0YQAvD_BwE [Accessed 26 Sep. 2023].
S C McCarthy and Leslie (n.d.) 2014 warmest year in modern record

2014 warmest year in modern record. [online] Climate Change: Vital Signs of the Planet. Available at: https://climate.nasa.gov/news/2221/2014-warmest-year-in-modern-record/.

NASA (2023) NASA says 2022 Fifth Warmest Year on Record, Warming Trend Continues [online] Climate Change: Vital Signs of the Planet. Available at: https://climate.nasa.gov/news/3246/nasa-says-2022-fifth-warmest-year-on-record-warming-trend-continues/.

Newsround (2023) 'Ulez: what is it and why is it so controversial?', BBC, 29 August.

Office for National Statistics (2018) The 2008 Recession 10 Years on – Office for National Statistics. [online] Ons.gov.uk. Available at: https://www.ons.gov.uk/economy/grossdomesticproductgdp/articles/the2008recession10yearson/2018-04-30.

press.un.orgditor, C.S., Whit. (2007). *SECURITY COUNCIL HOLDS FIRST-EVER DEBATE ON IMPACT OF CLIMATE CHANGE ON PEACE, SECURITY, HEARING OVER 50 SPEAKERS UN Press* [online] Available at: https://press.un.org/en/2007//sc900.doc.htm.

Chris Smyth (2023) 'Voters sceptical about climate pledges and cost, poll reveals', *The Times*, 26 September.

About the contributor

With a decade of expertise in data, data journalism, and marketing, Isabelle Marchand has crafted data visualisations for renowned organisations like The World Bank, Dropbox, the Ford Motor Company, Sainsbury's, and Lloyds Banking Group. She has co-written several books on data journalism and she frequently shares her insights at notable data events, including the Amsterdam Innovation Summit, Data Fest, and Data Summit.

Chapter 7

Mind the gap: public attitudes towards climate change

Most people in Britain are concerned about climate change. Nevertheless, some proposals for reducing carbon emissions are more popular than others, leaving scope for the issue to become divisive at the ballot box. Not least of the reasons for the difference between people's level of concern and their attitudes towards implementation is their reluctance to pay for the costs of transition. **Sir John Curtice** minds the figures

Concern about climate change is far from new. As long ago as 2005 Ipsos found as that as many as 82 per cent were concerned about the prospect, though by 2013 the figure had fallen to 60 per cent. Now, in their most recent reading, taken in July 2023, 77 per cent say they are 'very' or 'fairly' concerned. Indeed, in a number of readings taken over the last four years, the proportion has never been less than 76 per cent, while it reached a peak of 85 per cent in the immediate wake of the record heatwave that the UK experienced in July 2022. Similarly, the latest summer 2023 instalment of the regular public attitudes survey commissioned by the UK Department for Energy Security and Net Zero found that 82 per cent are 'very' or 'fairly' concerned about climate change.

Not just the young care

Contrary to many a journalistic cliché, concern about climate change is not especially high among younger people. According to Ipsos, the proportion of those aged under 35 who are concerned is, at 76 per cent, exactly the same proportion as among those aged 55 and over. Meanwhile, the UK's Department of Energy Security's most recent survey found that 46 per cent of those aged 65 and over are 'very' concerned about climate change, higher than in any other age group. While a demonstration or march about climate change might provide useful images for a media story, the age profile of those who are willing and able to attend is not necessarily a good guide to the pattern of public opinion. Rather, in so far as there are differences in the level of concern, they are to be found between graduates (more concerned) and those with few, if any, educational qualifications (less concerned), and between Conservative (less concerned) and Labour (more concerned) supporters – a point to which we will return.

There is also widespread agreement that global warming is at least in part the result of human actions. For example, when asked about the cause of the hot weather across much of continental Europe in summer 2023, 35 per cent said to Ipsos that it was 'mainly caused by climate change as a result of human activity' while another 47 per cent said that it was partly caused by human activity. According to Public First, approaching half (46 per cent) believe that climate change is the most serious threat facing the world. Consequently, it is not surprising that there is widespread support for the government's goal of reaching net zero (in terms of carbon emissions) by 2050. For example, 71 per cent told YouGov in July 2023 that they supported this aim, while just 20per cent were opposed. Meanwhile, in response to a more nuanced question posed by Public First for the Onward think tank in August 2023, 61 per cent said that the UK should aim to achieve net zero by 2050 or earlier, while only one in four (25 per cent) reckoned the target year should either be delayed or the goal abandoned entirely.

What is to be done?

Against this backdrop it is not surprising that many of the measures that could be taken to reduce carbon emission are relatively popular. However, that is by no means true of all of them. This is illustrated by our table below, which collates the pattern of responses from a number of recent polls to paint a picture of which possible steps are more or less popular.

Two approaches are broadly popular. The first is switching to renewable power, such as wind farms. Although onshore farms are a little less popular than offshore ones, voters have, it seems, largely embraced a technology that already provides a significant proportion of the UK's electricity supply. Whatever their visual impact, they offer, of course, the prospect of continued access to a familiar source of light and power. The second is making transition cheaper, either through subsidies or tax cuts for householders who are taking steps to make their homes more energy efficient. Voters are willing to be incentivised to make the transition.

However, as the entries in the bottom half of the table illustrate, increasing the taxes paid by individuals for activities that give rise to carbon emissions is largely unpopular. People are reluctant to see themselves priced out of accessing the goods and services that they enjoy – though they are happy to see taxation being used to encourage companies to reduce their emissions in providing the things their customers want to buy. That, of course, places the onus for change elsewhere.

	All Voters		Conservative supporters		Labour supporters	
	Support %	Oppose %	Support %	Oppose %	Support %	Oppose %
Subsidies to make homes more energy efficient	85	7	85	10	89	6
Tax companies with substantial carbon emissions	80	9	79	13	86	7
More offshore wind farms	70	7	71	8	72	9
Reduce VAT on energy efficiency improvements	62	7	66	7	68	7
More onshore wind farms	61	10	59	14	69	10
Build more nuclear power stations	49	32	63	23	43	38
Increase tax on long haul flights	47	41	43	50	56	30
Ban new gas boilers from 2035	42	37	26	56	58	22
Ban new petrol and diesel cars from 2030	38	43	31	61	53	34
Increase cost of air fares by 50per cent	29	56	28	59	33	53
Increase petrol tax	25	65	15	78	35	55
New tax on gas	16	71	8	86	21	65

Table: Attitudes towards possible climate change measures

Sources: More in Common, September 2023; Public First/Onward, August 2023; YouGov, April 2023; YouGov/Times, August 2023

In contrast, when asked about steps that involve changing the infrastructure of how we acquire and consume energy, public opinion appears to be evenly balanced. Both attitudes towards banning the sale of gas boilers (and thus, most likely, pushing households towards a heat pump as their source of heating) and the sale of petrol and diesel cars (with the expectation that drivers switch to electric cars) fall into that category. The same is true of expanding the use of nuclear power, which, although not a new technology, is one that has long been controversial because of its perceived environmental risks. It is these more profound changes to the production and consumption of energy, some of which will have a direct impact on people's day to day lives, where there is the greatest potential for debate and controversy.

Where is the divide/the wedge?

These are also the steps that are potentially most electorally divisive. As well as showing the distribution of attitudes, our table also shows separately the views of those who voted Conservative and Labour in 2019. In the case of the most popular measures there is relatively little difference between them. However, otherwise, the somewhat lower concern about climate change among Conservative supporters is accompanied by a somewhat greater reluctance to support any particular measure – apart, that is, from greater use of nuclear power, where longstanding debates about its environmental safety still leave their imprint. The gap is particularly large in respect of the eventual banning of gas boilers and of petrol and diesel cars, thereby perhaps helping to explain why in September 2023 the Conservative government opted to scale back some of its plans for these measures. Despite the political consensus about much of climate change, there is clearly scope for its implementation to become something of an electoral dividing line between the parties.

Combatting climate change . . . but at what price?

In any event, there is a considerable gap between people's level of concern about climate change and their willingness to support measures that might stop the warming of the planet. As we might already anticipate, perceived cost appears to be a significant barrier. Although Ipsos found that 41 per cent believe that not dealing with climate change will be more expensive than the cost of addressing it, while only 22 per cent take the opposite view, paying for climate change measures appears to be an important consideration for a public that is currently having to cope with an inflationary spiral. In 2022, only 13 per cent told YouGov that addressing climate change was a bigger priority than dealing with climate change. The following July, over half (55 per cent) said that 'policies to reduce carbon emissions should only be introduced if they do not result in additional costs for ordinary people', while just 27per cent expressed the opposite view. Similarly, Ipsos found in September 2023 that 51 per cent would like to do more to reduce climate change but could not afford to, with just 19 per cent disagreeing. Meanwhile, the Department of Energy Security's summer 2023 survey found that as many as 69 per cent believe that the transition to net zero will increase their regular living expenses in the short term, while 48 per cent also reckon this is true of the longer term. The claim of some campaigners that addressing climate change will be economically beneficial is doubted by many voters.

But if there is a cost, upon whom should it fall - on individuals or on society as a whole? This too is a subject on which the public are divided. According to Public First's poll for Onward, 43 per cent believe that the costs of transition should wholly or mainly be met by individuals, while 46 per cent reckon that most or all of the cost should be funded by government. Conservative voters (54 per cent) are somewhat keener than Labour supporters (42 per cent) on the government bearing most of the cost. Presumably their lower level of enthusiasm for some measures in the first place means Conservatives take the view that if change has to be implemented then they should not have to bear the costs – and that this outlook cuts across their traditional preference for less government spending.

Climate change is there but not for me?

Against this backdrop, it is perhaps little wonder that YouGov have consistently found that around half of voters think the government is not doing enough to reduce carbon emissions. For it looks as though many voters, of all political persuasions, are hoping that climate change will be addressed by government action, and that in the meantime they will largely be able to carry on with their lives as usual. Of course, the crucial question is whether this attitude will prove realistic.

About the contributor

Professor Sir John Curtice is President of the British Polling Council, a Professor of Politics at the University of Strathclyde, and a senior research fellow at the National Centre for Social Research and 'The UK in a Changing Europe'. A regular contributor to BBC election night programmes, he is also co-host of the Trendy podcast.

SECTION THREE

The British media and climate change

Introduction

Andrew Beck

The British media has a chequered history as far as climate change is concerned. By turns it has sidelined it, blown it up to apocalyptic heights, and equivocated about it. Newspaper front pages and TV news headlines have featured stark images of a burning planet. Equally so, newspaper op-ed pages have given space to climate change sceptics and deniers. Where once the topic might have been governed by the spirit of scientific discovery, now it has become a key battleground in contemporary culture wars. For Brexit now read climate change scepticism. Indeed, Matthew d'Ancona has traced the transformation of Euroscepticism into eco-scepticism as a powerful political voice in British media and politics.

Despite sales of print editions of newspapers falling worldwide, their front pages, their editorials, and their star columnists still wield considerable influence. Late night TV news programmes always feature a round-up of the next days' newspapers' front pages, and breakfast TV programmes offer similar surveys. Newspaper ownership is still a highly prized business objective as newspaper owners can exert enormous influence over their titles' contents, often to the dismay of those titles' journalists trying their best to walk a narrow line between fact, reasonable comment, and overt ideology.

This section begins and ends with contributions from former *Times* executive Liz Gerard. In 2020 she addressed the question 'Is Fleet Street in climate change denial?' (Although British newspapers have long since moved from the central London location of Fleet Street, the term persists as a metonym for the press.) Analysing historic newspaper coverage of climate change she offers incisive assessment, as well as revealing personal anecdotes, from the front line of newspaper production. From her 2020 survey and reflections she found newspapers out of touch not only in what they reported but also in how they presented themselves: 'They seem to be floundering, both editorially and commercially – still wrapping their weekend magazines in unrecyclable plastic bags to accommodate all the junk leaflets (some themselves wrapped in plastic) that readers throw away without a glance'.

Ted Young is another Fleet Street veteran. In 'Inconvenient truth: the press and climate change' he reflects on his years in the trade with especial reference to climate change reporting. He offers a balanced and nuanced account of the difficult job the press has in terms of reporting climate change, calling out climate change hypocrisy where it occurs, and giving a voice to people who, however sympathetic they might be to green causes, are still angry when they can't get to work because of climate change demonstrations. So febrile is the atmosphere of climate change debate that genuinely objective journalistic investigations into the mining of, for example, cobalt, manganese, nickel, and graphite, are treated as anti-green treatises. Young proudly stakes a claim for what he regards as the objective stance of the news providers, not taking sides but calling out both sides: 'it's only natural the press should take aim at double standards when it comes to climate change'.

Whilst newspaper sales and readership figures are tumbling, and the proliferation of TV channels has led to audience fragmentation, there are plenty of new and different opportunities for newsgathering and dissemination. In 'Phones for the future: filming climate campaigns on my mobile' videojournalist Zoe Broughton writes about how she was able to launch and maintain a career in climate change campaign reporting using only her mobile phone: 'I am now celebrating being a video journalist for 30 years. I specialise in covering protests and direct actions. Currently nearly all my projects are linked to the greatest threat our humanity has faced, that of the climate emergency'. Broughton not only recounts stories from the front line of climate change protest reporting but also offers insights into how modern lightweight technology has revolutionised alternative means of telling the news. Where once she used 'one expensive suite' to edit material sent out on VHS tapes, now she trains 'folk in how to record and edit good footage on their phones, and of course there is the internet to share your media'.

Whilst newspaper front page images and TV news lead items of climate change havoc and banner headlines announcing the latest climate disaster tell undeniable truths they can be tremendously upsetting. What is often missing from any media discussion about climate change is the eco-anxiety ordinary people feel when confronted with what appear to be insuperable forces. In 'A future for the climate: devolution and participation in climate documentaries' Dr Elke Weissmann and Belinda Tyrrell write about that very eco-anxiety, and explore ways and means they, as media production teachers, have used to counterbalance despair with hope and inspiration. As they assert, 'the reporting of climate change as disasters needs to be balanced with stories of local communities already doing their bit'. Describing how their work not only had positive impacts on the communities with which they worked, they also report on the positive changes that work had on them. Realising that didactic teaching modes would not work in these contexts, they show how their moving to more collaborative teaching methods made for cooperative and complementary working practices. They conclude: 'local communities are already doing a lot, and they are very good at articulating the variety of benefits to their actions [...] It is by representing both the co-benefits of climate action and "the little things" that people can do, that others, who are currently not doing a lot, can be inspired'.

BBC News and Current Affairs climate change reporting comes in for a lot of very partial coverage, not to say overt criticism, by newspapers such as *The Express*, *The Mail*, *The Sun*, and *The Telegraph*, as well as new TV stations such as GB News and TalkTV. Dubbed the British Bashing Corporation by Dan Wootton at the time of King Charles III's coronation, the facts of the matter of the Corporation are rarely, if ever, examined. BBC critics are often content to cherry-pick one quotation and to extrapolate from that a whole ideological platform. That said, Media Studies has occasionally been guilty of equally selective practices when lambasting Corporation critics. But there is a long and noble tradition of content analysis in Communication and Media Studies, dating back to the pioneering 1920s work of Harold Lasswell. In 'BBC News and Current Affairs: a climate change case study' Professor Stephen Cushion reports on an exhaustive study of BBC output on this topic. Taking three weeks in June 2019, Cushion and his Cardiff University research team applied themselves to a staggering amount of BBC output. Given that the media marketplace for news is an 'increasingly crowded and competitive media marketplace' he begins by readily accepting that genuine 'concerns have understandably been raised about the range and depth of programming available in today's news ecology' and in particular about the BBC. Scrupulously analysing that output, and offering comparative analysis of newscasting by ITV, Channel 4, and Channel 5, he concludes that the BBC did not stand alone in its coverage of climate change, nor was it unique in challenging government claims: 'With the exception of Heart and Channel 5, all news providers challenged the government's claims, either directly by a journalist or by referring to a direct or indirect source'.

And so back to Liz Gerard. Three years after her 2020 survey of British newspapers' climate coverage Liz Gerard returned to the topic to ask 'Is Fleet Street still in climate change denial?' Her short answer is yes. While she does salute some titles for their serious coverage of the subject, she laments many newspapers' positive reaction to Rishi Sunak's U-turn on climate change measures: 'much of the press and many MPs remain in denial, urging the Government to abandon or shelve net zero measures and green taxes'. And while some front pages show the planet burning too many politicians and too many newspapers not only ignore measures to bring about net zero but also rejoice in their being junked: 'it's on with the blinkers for right-wing politicians and press. Fire up the gas boiler, fill the tank with diesel and be merry, for tomorrow we die'.

Reference

Matthew d'Ancona (2023) 'The Eurosceptics are now ecosceptics .. this time, they will wreck the planet' *The New European*, 17-25 August.

About the contributor

Andrew Beck is co-editor of *Toxic News*.

Chapter 8

Is Fleet Street in climate change denial?

In 2020 **Liz Gerard** examined UK newspaper coverage of climate change. She concluded they looked out of touch, out of date, and out of ideas

As a late-night editor, you get used to being blamed in absentia in the morning-after inquests. Often you will learn of your trial and conviction, third-hand, days later, since by the time you report for work next afternoon, everyone has moved on and is focused on tomorrow's paper. So, few of these sins stick in the memory.

One, however, is as clear as day twenty years on. Not least because it involved a totally unexpected full-scale carpeting from an embarrassed acting editor. Summoned to the editor's suite the moment I arrived in the office, I was told: "We have a problem with the way you rewrote the splash this morning."

"But I didn't rewrite it."

"You did. I have the history [the electronic paper trail showing the various changes in copy from the moment the file is created to the published article]."

It had to be serious to go to such efforts. The story was about climate change, a warning about global warming. Just one or two words had been juggled but the effect, in the editor's eyes, was devastating. The story accepted that global warming was a fact.

"But it is," I said. "Yes," said he. "But this story suggests that it is man-made. The science doesn't back that up."

I was still perplexed. What was the big deal?

"This is the one thing that really gets the proprietor going."

Ah. There had clearly been a phone call. The proprietor might not interfere in day-to-day editorial decision-making, but if something was plain wrong, well . . .

The proprietor was, of course, Rupert Murdoch. And, even though the science does now back up the man-made argument, his views – or perceived views - on climate change don't seem to have changed that much.

Don't mention the climate

By 2019 any Murdoch-induced climate scepticism seemed to be dissipating among his titles, if not necessarily among his columnists. In March 2019 the World Meteorological Organisation reported that in 2018, 62m people had been affected and nearly 2,000 killed by devastating floods, fires, storms, and heatwaves that it put down to climate change. *The Sun* gave the story six pars on page 2, alongside a report that sunseekers in Britain would be 'enjoying' a day hotter than the Med, a bright daffodil picture, and a very sunny three-day forecast. It was left to readers to decide whether to make the connection the juxtaposition implied.

The Times carried the climate report as a nib on a world news page. No one else touched it. Well, it was supposed to be Brexit day. Maybe they had other fish to fry. Next day, *The Times*'s Irish edition followed up with an op-ed headlined, 'As we rubberneck Brexit, our planet is dying'.

In 2018 we saw wildfires ravage California, Brazil, and Australia; in Britain, summer temperatures soared, and thousands have had their homes wrecked by flooding. Every December, we are told that this year has been hotter than the last. The evidence is everywhere. What's more, it matters to voters – i.e. readers – so that it ranked ahead of immigration in pre-election 'issues affecting the country' polls. One BBC producer working with young audiences told me that only two issues mattered to the under-30s: climate change and Brexit. In that order. 'Climate strike' was *Collins Dictionary*'s word of the year, while the *OED* went for 'climate emergency'.

Yet print news coverage remains scant, so that even 62 million people being affected by climate-driven catastrophes or statistics showing that the 2010s were the hottest decade on record cannot find their way into many papers.

The March 2020 'hottest decade' report from the UN led the main television news bulletins, but a basement on page 4 in the *FT* and an 18-19 spread in the *Guardian* were the best treatment it received in the press. *The Express*, which splashed for the second day on whether Big Ben should 'bong' for Brexit, did not give it a sentence. And among those that did find space for the story, there was absolutely no joined-up thinking. Not one paper tied the report to coverage of David Attenborough puffing a new 'people threaten the planet' programme – or to the fallout from Storm Brendan. All three were kept completely separate, pages apart.

This was all par for the course. We see an obligatory nod to global warming in reports of the foreign wildfires, but not in those of the flooding here. We read about the way people's homes have been destroyed, their lives disrupted, telephone-number tolls of animals killed – as indeed we should – but where is the background, an examination of the Australian coal-mining industry, for example? The standard response is a Q&A panel, kissing off the environmental policy element in five sentences.

Even when climate was put centre stage in a televised debate during the 2019 UK general election campaign, coverage focused not on rival policies but on melting ice sculptures and Michael Gove trying to invite himself on to the programme. The prime minister's father got more news space and airtime from that event than the planet. We should have been reading about fracking, wind farms, and nuclear energy; instead we were offered 'media bias' and a threat to Channel 4's licence.

A forest of trees must have been felled to provide the newsprint devoted to decrying Extinction Rebellion and the disruption their protests caused, but what of the February 2020 climate summit in Madrid? Barely a word – apart from Greta, of course.

Greta Thunberg is a phenomenon. Here we have a 16-year-old girl who in less than a year has single-handedly motivated her generation to action, met world leaders (apart from Theresa May), addressed conferences and been named the youngest *Time* magazine person of the year.

The last teenager to make that sort of impact was Malala Yousafzai, the Pakistani Nobel peace laureate who fought for girls' right to an education. She was lauded all over the world, the subject of admiring profiles in every paper.

Saint or shrew?

But not Greta. 'Woke' papers like the *Guardian*, *Observer*, *FT* and *Independent* have carried in-depth features, but for the rest, the attitude towards this young woman is epitomised by this sentence from the *Mail*'s Stephen Glover: "Now I have no wish to criticise a brave and resourceful campaigner whose heart is in the right place, but . . ."

Always the 'but'. And, sometimes, not even the positive sweetener first. Some of the headlines make you wince: 'The disturbing spectacle of Greta the Great', 'I don't need Greta's lectures', 'Teenagers should ignore Greta's sermons', 'Greta's glam mummy – and a climate of suspicion', 'The gospel according to 'saint' Greta', 'Labour needs a leader who's prepared to kill terrorists – and doesn't bang on about Greta Thunberg'. There is something deeply unsavoury about powerful sixty-something men hectoring a girl young enough to be their granddaughter – a child, for heaven's sake – from the safety of their keyboards in their cosy offices while she's sailing across the Atlantic. At least the *Sun*'s *Fabulous* magazine named her as one of its women of the year.

Greta is far from alone in receiving this treatment. For while most papers now accept there is a problem with the climate, there is still plenty of bile for those who want to do something about it. Especially if they are royals – or, rather, Harry and Meghan – or 'luvvies' – particularly Emma Thompson – since their every flight can be cited as proof of their 'holier-than-thou hypocrisy'.

And 'banging on' is their greatest crime.

Not just about plastic bags

So, voters care about it. Readers care about it. But how should newspapers feed this growing appetite? More stories about melting glaciers, suicidal walruses, boiling kelp, and burnt koalas? Would that not depress people more and make them feel even more impotent? (There is a rich seam of stories about young people taking anti-depressants to combat their despair over the planet). Vegan recipes and more campaigns to persuade supermarkets to reduce packaging?

Individuals all over the country are making small stands – from Veganuary and unpacking shopping at the checkout (forcing the supermarket to deal with the plastic), to swapping clingfilm for beeswax, and giving up buying new. There are more stories out there than charging for plastic bags, but they're not being picked up and developed. Our newspapers look out of touch, out of date and out of ideas. They seem to be floundering, both editorially and commercially – still wrapping their weekend magazines in unrecyclable plastic bags to accommodate all the junk leaflets (some themselves wrapped in plastic) that readers throw away without a glance.

If you aren't making that basic change yourself and half your columnists are mocking 'eco warriors' for wanting to squeeze every drop of joy from your life, it doesn't really work to say, 'this is what you can do'. And, as they keep pointing out, Britain is ahead of many countries in seeking to reduce emissions. The real environmental villains are far bigger, far more powerful, and far out of earshot of British tabloid readers.

I asked a handful of science writers what the press should be doing. The answers were not encouraging. Few were willing to speak – "I can't be seen telling the media what to do," said one – and none was prepared to go on the record.

"Climate change is a massive problem," another said. "For a long time, sceptics sort of let us all off. We could show our virtue by disagreeing with them – and ignore the fact that we were all flying and driving too. Now they are increasingly being ignored. I don't know what the press's role is in this; basically because I'm not sure what anyone's is. We're all screwed."

This chapter is an edited version of Liz Gerard's 2 March 2020 *InPublishing* column.

About the contributor

Liz Gerard is a former *The Times* executive. She monitors the UK daily national press and reports on it acerbically and in depth for *InPublishing* fortnightly.

Chapter 9

Inconvenient truth: the press and climate change

The British press often comes in for criticism over its reporting of climate change. Former tabloid editor **Ted Young** says mainstream media can sometimes be the victim of fake news

'It's a mainstream media conspiracy.'

'Climate change should be on the front page every day, the top of every news agenda. They are just ignoring the crisis facing the world today.'

These are views I hear, time and again, and sometimes I've really had to take them on the nose.

Stepping gingerly around a stinking pile of manure dumped by Extinction Rebellion protesters outside my newspaper office in High Street Kensington a couple of years ago, I was, along with fellow journalists, the target of their ire. Their banner proclaimed 'Free the Press'.

This seemed a little ironic considering climate change protesters just a year before had blockaded our print works to prevent papers getting out to the British public.

But I've been a journalist for 40 years. Bankers had a go when the Press dared to question their massive bonuses after the credit crunch. Politicians moaned when their vast expenses claims (one for a duck house) were exposed and, more recently, when the utter hypocrisy of those in power was laid bare by the Downing Street lockdown parties. So it's only natural the press should take aim at double standards when it comes to climate change.

Preach

It was a bit rich when Prince Harry attended the Google Camp in Sicily back in 2019 after flying in by private jet to preach to us all, barefoot on a beach, about saving the planet. He was in good company as more than 100 other non-commercial flights flew in to attend the event.

Even King Charles, a frontrunner in raising the alarm about climate change, has come under fire for arranging for four cabinet ministers to fly up to see him for a Net Zero meeting in Scotland. Has anyone told His Majesty about Zoom?

Meanwhile Rishi Sunak appears barely able to go to the shops without taking a helicopter. But it's still 'damn the mainstream media'. We are rude enough to prick the bubble, to call out hypocrisy.

At *Metro* newspaper, when I was editor, we had the temerity to do it again in 2021 when we pointed out that billionaires Bill Gates and Jeff Bezos had been partying on their gas-guzzling superyachts in the run-up to COP26.

Chilling

Mr Gates landed in Glasgow after 'chilling' on his rental gin palace that pumps out an estimated 7,000 tons of carbon dioxide a year. He arranged a fleet of helicopters to ferry guests from his yacht to his 66th birthday bash on the Turkish coast. Mr Bezos took a 120-mile round trip from his £290million floating mansion to the Gates party before jetting 2,000 miles to COP26 on his £48million Gulf Stream jet. Some 400 of the world's elite flew private to Glasgow.

So why does this matter? It matters because to the ordinary punter, the commuter heading to work just making ends meet, it seems a little much to be lectured on 'doing your bit for the planet' and 'don't fly for your holidays' as the world's elite do the very opposite.

As my headline at *Metro* put it: The Height Of HyCOPrisy.

And it matters to me as a parent and grandparent who cares very deeply about climate change.

I believe the planet IS facing an existential crisis.

Doomsday

Why else did *Metro*, Britain's biggest tabloid, carry the front page headline 'Code Red For Humanity' in

August 2021 as we reported the Doomsday UN report on global warming? That is far from burying bad news.

And when the US President, leader of the Western World, didn't turn up for the G7 Climate Change conference in 2019 our banner headline screamed 'What Planet Is Trump On?' It was a wipeout front page again for us in April 2021 with the headline '... The Planet's had enough hot air, it's ... Time To Step Up'. This was President Biden's message, delivered virtually (with minimal carbon footprint) because of Covid.

Crikey, so the press DOES report the climate crisis. I'm not saying by any means that the mainstream media is perfect. It riles me to see 'so much for global warming' headlines as soon as the temperatures plunge or there is an inch of snow.

But the British press has also done great work. The huge success of the *Daily Mail's* 'Turn the tide on plastic' campaign should not be underestimated. At *Metro* we always called out double standards. *Metro* readers are a very mixed bunch, a good cross-section of Britain's workforce.

Many supported the climate change protests, many did not. But if they are on the Docklands Light Railway trying to get to work and a climate change activist glues themselves to their carriage, they are not amused. These are commuters who are not driving in, causing minimal damage to the planet but who are targeted because they are an easy way to get publicity. Similarly, if an ambulance is trying to get to hospital but is blocked by Just Stop Oil protesters, there is real anger against people who believe they are right and everyone else is wrong.

Damage

The press is right to question everything. What is the cost of shifting from using fossil fuel to electricity? Or indeed the cost of not doing this in the long term.

Where does the iron come from? Where does the copper come from? Vast quantities are needed to make the change from fossil fuel. What is the damage mining does to the local environment? What is the carbon footprint?

What is the real cost of wind turbines? What harm do they cause to bird life and wildlife in general? Nothing compared with farming, it is argued. But are they ruining our countryside? Should they just be built offshore?

Electric cars. How green are they? Volvo has said the emissions from the production of electric cars are far higher than a petrol equivalent. Is this true? And what about the carbon cost of scrapping cars? These are the complex questions facing decision-makers. A real paradox.

Because you ask these questions does not mean you are a swivel-eyed reactionary. In the Twittersphere (now X-sphere) just putting your head above the parapet and saying anything against the perceived wisdom is becoming more risky than an owl taking on a turbine blade.

Harsh

Channel 4 boss Alex Mahon recently said Generation Z can't work alongside people with different views and don't have the skills to debate post-pandemic. That may be harsh but it does appear we are going down a road where people only listen to the opinions of those with whom they agree.

Get it wrong in the press and the public can complain to the Independent Press Standards Organisation. If it's serious enough, a correction can appear on the front page or on a newspaper website's home page. Get it wrong on social media and nobody gives a fig.

Meanwhile there are spats in the hallowed halls of academia over whether prestigious science journal *Nature* selects climate papers that 'support certain pre-approved narratives'. That is the charge that is being made by Patrick T Brown at John Hopkins University. *Nature* has hit back sand accused the lecturer of 'poor research practices'.

It just goes to show that there is a war for hearts and minds across all levels of media. And that war is being fought now in the UK ahead of the 2024 General Election. Why is Prime Minister Rishi Sunak retreating on the Government's Net Zero targets?

Embrace

Is that the power of the press or is it because households simply can't afford the fast-paced move to green and Rishi wants their votes? I suspect it's the latter.

London Mayor Sadiq Khan's Ulez (ultra low emission zones) tax on drivers of older cars may well have lost his Labour party the by-election in Boris Johnson's old parliamentary seat in Uxbridge.

It's one thing calling for a greener planet and another thing paying for it. That is why honest debate and freedom of speech is so vital to get the public to embrace the green message. Because only then will readers and viewers be persuaded that they really can change the world.

Shouting at people on X and or lecturing them after flying in on your private jet to tell them only you know the answers will simply add fuel to the fire. And the planet will continue to burn.

About the contributor

Ted Young was *Metro* editor from 2014 to 2023. Before that he was editor of the *New York Daily News Online, Mail Online*, *London Lite*, executive editor at the *Daily Express*, and assistant editor at *The Sun*. He is a member of the Independent Press Standards complaints committee, and a non-executive director at Cover Media. Young has an MA in History from Cambridge University.

Chapter 10

Phones for the future: filming climate campaigns on my mobile

Video journalist **Zoe Broughton** writes about guerilla film-making of climate protests

It's October 2018. I keep hearing about a new climate campaign group called Extinction Rebellion (known as XR) and have secured a commission to film its launch in London.

The journalist and activist George Monbiot is going and I plan to follow him for the day. We cycle to the train station. He is pedaling his bike along the High Street in Oxford with old buildings passing by in the background. I am filming on my phone from the back of a tandem.

"We're heading off for Extinction Rebellion in London today, and it's about time," says George. "I've been working for 33 years on these issues, and we're not getting any respite from government, we're not getting any respite from industry so we've got to take this in to our own hands. Shut things down until we are listened to, until we start to get the kind of action which is commensurate with the scale of the problem and at the moment we could scarcely be further from that. So, this is where people power kicks in and hopefully it's the beginning of change."

On the train I quickly edit this video clip in my phone and post it to Twitter (now X). The event has not even started yet. He shares my tweet and the number of viewers shoots up. We run off several of these pieces to camera throughout that first XR day.

Celebrating 30 years of videojournalism

I am now celebrating being a video journalist for 30 years. I specialise in covering protests and direct actions. Currently nearly all my projects are linked to the greatest threat our humanity has faced, that of the climate emergency.

XR has now been active for five years with hundreds of groups around the globe. In the UK XR has three demands: to act now; to tell the truth; and the third demand is that the Government must create and be led by the decisions of a Citizens' Assembly on Climate and Ecological Justice. The XR protests are creative and spectacular.

During the COP25, Conference of the Parties, talks in Madrid I could not keep up with editing the multiple XR actions happening daily and so I used a new skill I had acquired, that of livestreaming. Livestreaming is filming directly to an online platform such as Facebook giving an immediate window on to what is happening.

On one of the final evenings at COP25 an XR group blocked the roundabout outside the conference centre. Tents popped up, musical instruments were played, and the protestors looked set to stay. I debated going back to my room to sleep or staying there. If the police did move in it would be good to witness this. Filming makes everyone accountable for their actions.

I ask if one of the tents can squeeze another person in and I lie on the cardboard covered floor, my head on my camera bag. Despite the cold I did fall asleep for a couple of hours and woke to shouting. The riot police had arrived.

I start the livestream as I push my way out of the tent and into the chaos. Spanish police are clad in uniforms that make them look like they are from a sci-fi film, with bright lights and cold steamy breath. Individually they do not communicate but a tannoy message announces all must leave and the police start dragging and carrying those who refuse.

Making it live

Over the following months a group of us work on improving our livestream skills and equipment. A tech specialist, called Vlad Morozov learns software so we can multi camera livestream with up to eight video inputs - usually these are people recording on their phones, filming from anywhere in the world directly into one livestream. He live edits between the different cameras from his home and can also add pre-recorded films. This is then streamed to multiple different social media platforms such as Twitter, YouTube, and Facebook simultaneously, resulting in slick productions on an extremely low budget to a wide global audience.

Back in the UK and there is another wave of XR actions across the capital. We use the multi camera set up and I am hovering around Parliament Square waiting for something to start. I am briefly caught out by a decoy. A loud woman stands on the grass square and yells about the climate emergency whilst peeling off her t-shirt and she then holds up a placard. The police move to arrest her. Whilst this is happening 15 other women have quietly stripped to their waists with messages stenciled on their bodies: WAR, PANDEMIC, STARVATION. Using bike locks they have attached their necks to the fence surrounding Parliament.

I rush towards them panning along their topless torsos and interviewing some of them about the purpose of their action before I have to leave the police cordon. Viewing numbers reached over three million. 'Bare the Truth 'is the title of their press release. Three million people interested in their demands about the climate crisis, or just watching to see their breasts?

Back in the 1990s I was a co-founder of *Undercurrents*, a video magazine covering direct actions from across the globe. *The Guardian* described us as 'The news you don't see on the news', and our 'video magazine offers the environmental and social justice film footage the other TV channels won't show'. Sadly for many mainstream broadcast media this hasn't changed.

But the technology has. We had one expensive edit suite to use for the whole of the *Undercurrents* team and we distributed the videos on VHS tapes which we were posting out. Now I train folk in how to record and edit good footage on their phones, and of course there is the internet to share your media.

One of the stranger film requests I had was by a vicar who calls me up asking if I'll film him sewing up his lips because, he says, "Climate science and truth has been muted, those who suffer are not being heard."

I team up with a filmmaker, Dave Tarvit, for this project. Obviously Tim won't be able to talk through this action so we pre-record an interview and Dave cuts this together with archive footage of climate disasters.

"I am the reverend Tim Hewes, I'm aged 71 and I'll be sewing up my lips to demonstrate the terrible havoc Murdoch's actions have wreaked upon the world and symbolically make visible this truth.

"Murdoch has been a climate change denier for decades. He's suppressed a wealth of evidence based, peer reviewed, scientific observation from thousands of preeminent scientists from around the globe.'

"He has ridiculed and attempted to discredit the warnings of highly regarded humanity agencies and eminent ambassadors and activists for the planet."

Dave has the edit ready early that morning so he can simply drop in the shots of the sewing protest as soon as the deed is done.

It is hard to film as Tim repeatedly forces the large needle through his flesh creating a crooked zigzag and stands outside the News UK's office in Central London.

After the action Tim removes the stitching and we go to sit with others in a nearby cafe. Dave sends the final

edit of this rather gruesome film through and, grimacing, we watch it on my phone.

Peckish now, after an early start, I buy some salty crisps and popcorn, ripping open the packets and putting them on the table to share. Tim, without thinking, takes a handful and the pain kicks in, the adrenalin has gone and salt touches the holes where there had just been thick waxed thread. Sorry Tim!

Filming Just Stop Oil

Another group now keeping me busy is Just Stop Oil who currently have just one demand! They want there to be no new oil licenses granted. On 19 September Sunak watered down the government's Net Zero plans and soon after gave the go-ahead to the UK's largest new oilfield, Rosebank. At this crucial time are we heading in completely the wrong direction?

In October 2022 I was filming a Just Stop Oil march blocking a London bridge. I've probably filmed close on two hours of footage that day. As I am flipping through this on my phone I choose and edit a clip of a woman being carried along face down by the police. I had dashed alongside. "Is there anything you want to say to camera?" I asked.

She lifted her head and looked into the lens. "I'm doing this for my son," she said. "The government's inaction on climate change is a death sentence to us all. The United Nations have said we should have no new oil. Liz Truss wants to open a 130 new oil licences. That's a death sentence to this planet."

The film is just 15 seconds long. The colours are amazing: long auburn hair, an orange t-shirt, the police in their hi viz uniforms.

Going viral

George Monbiot and comedian Ricky Gervais share my tweet. There is a dopamine hit seeing the viewing numbers rise each time I refresh the page. I celebrate with a bottle of beer as it hits 1 million views. By the next morning it had jumped to over 11 million.

A few weeks later I meet up with Lora, the woman in the video. She has a court hearing in London. We head to a cafe and look for a table near an electrical socket because she needs to charge up her ankle tag, the result of taking part in several climate actions.

On Boxing Day I notice that my video of her has more views than the King's Christmas speech on BBC iPlayer.

If I hadn't filmed that clip on my phone, would those scrolling Twitter have seen her action that day? It's the same with the million views on my TikTok channel. It was also shared to Al-Jazeera's Instagram, and seen across America on the news programme *The Majority Report.* Even the BBC published an article with the title 'Suffolk protester's arrest viewed more than 11 million times'.

You could do this too. My current film kit comprises my phone with a Gimbal to steady the footage, and I have good radio mics, but you can just use your phone.

My eyes are wide open to our impending future. I am trying not to let fear overwhelm me, fear of what our heating world is rushing towards. On a personal level I am shocked that it is not constantly our main conversation. My hope is that everyone acts on this crisis using the skills that they have, and this means journalists and editors of all media prioritising their coverage of the climate emergency.

Meeting Greta

At that first Extinction Rebellion event I met Greta Thunberg. I had already followed her on Twitter and she followed me back. This was shortly before she became a global icon. I filmed her talk in Parliament Square.

"I remember thinking it was very strange, that humans are an animal species among others, could be capable of changing the world's climate, because if we were and if it was really happening, we wouldn't be talking about anything else. As soon as you turned on the TV, everything would be about that, headlines, radio, newspapers.

"They say climate change is an existential threat and yet they just carry on as before."

This speech, given by a 15-year-old, is seared into my memory. She ended with:

"So everyone out there, it is time for civil disobedience, it is time to rebel."

About the contributor

Zoe Broughton is an Oxford-based freelance video journalist, livestreamer, camera operator, social media content maker, video editor, and film tutor. She is currently working on her first book.

Chapter 11

A future for the climate: devolution and participation in climate documentaries

Climate change is often reported in the context of wildfires and floods. **Dr Elke Weissmann** and **Belinda Tyrrell** argue that, unfortunately, the persistent focus on disasters can lead to eco-anxiety. As a counterbalance reports of community climate action can give hope and inspire others to do more

Climate change as disaster

Horrendous wildfires in Greece, apocalyptic downpours in Libya. Unless you have managed to hide under a rock, you must be aware of the ever-increasing frequency of catastrophic climate events. Climate disasters are so frequent now that it can feel as if one is immediately following the next, so that the disasters push each other out of the headlines. Climate change becomes harder to deny in the light of these catastrophes. But psychologists (Whitmarsh et al. 2022; Vakoch and Mickey 2022) have found that the constant stream of news about climate disasters is not conducive to us changing our behaviour because it can cause eco-anxiety which can lead to paralysis (Heeren et al. 2022; Innocenti et al. 2023): we are frozen in fear as we see the world burn and/or drown around us.

Joseph Rehling (2022) compares the dread of climate anxiety with our existential fear of dying. He argues that this may explain why so many of us continue as if nothing had happened. But we want to contest this: is it true that so many of us do nothing? If we believe media reporting, then perhaps yes. Apart from *Gardeners' World* (BBC, 1968 - present) and *Countryfile* (BBC, 1988 - present) which occasionally present us with individual or community projects that are focused on sustainability and wildlife conservation, very few stories of everyday climate action circulate in the media. But many of us are already doing their bit: be that by shopping environmentally consciously, for example by buying as much local produce as possible, by diligently recycling, by walking or cycling or taking public transport, by shifting to green energy providers, installing solar panels or heat pumps, and so on. And some of us do significantly more.

Reporting climate action through collaboration

What could be the impact if more of these actions were reported? What would happen if the media responded to a populace who already consider that the environment is the fourth most important topic that politicians need to address (YouGov, 2023)? These are questions that emerged as we conducted research on a number of local community groups in Liverpool, UK, and we here want to share some of our findings. Let's be honest, though: we approached our project by asking ourselves how we can get ordinary people to change their behaviour. But then we realised that rather than approaching communities like a teacher, didactically, as so much reporting does, we should see ourselves as collaborators with skills that can complement those of the community.

Our skills were those of media production: we worked with our students to make short documentaries about four climate assemblies and four local community groups. These were not skills our community groups were interested in developing. They had enough on their plates with their projects and were glad that we could make a programme about them which they could use to publicise their work. This points to the need to rethink some of the rhetoric about participation and media. While we can, theoretically, now all produce our own media content and have, as a result, become prosumers (Ritzer and Jurgenson, 2010), we don't all want to. There are other things that may seem more important in our quest to keep the planet habitable.

It's not just the climate, stupid

One example of these other things is the education and support for inexperienced cyclists that Aigburth Community Cycle Club, one of our community groups, offers. Other groups included an in Bloom group that gardened with an environmental consciousness, a litter picking group, and the Love Wavertree food club which uses food waste from the supermarkets to feed the local community. Aigburth Community Cycle Club was founded in 2021 and leads community rides to help develop confidence in new cyclists. We followed one of their rides, and interviewed both the ride leaders and the group members who came along.

A quick search of some news and television databases shows that there are relatively few stories about cycling in the British press or on television. In the press, cycling is usually mentioned in relation to road safety, often in the context of the death or serious injury of a cyclist in an accident. This makes cycling appear dangerous. Other cycling stories focus on professional cycling, thus creating a frame of sports and leisure rather than suggesting that cycling is a means of transport. The sports frame is the most prevalent on television where reporting about cycling is largely confined to cycle races or recreational events.

In our interviews, cycling for leisure was also a key feature but it wasn't the only one. Our participants highlighted a number of benefits which included exercise and physical and mental health. In addition, they also suggested that cycling was cheaper than running a car, that it was faster than walking, and that it was environmentally more friendly than driving. The ride members also described driving as stressful, whereas they didn't think cycling was. Thus, the short programme made visible that cycling is a form of transport, and that it comes with a number of co-benefits, including the reduction of costs, improvement of physical and mental health, to those able to cycle. The participants' clear articulation of the benefits of cycling highlights that providing the space for the community to express why they are involved in climate action can lead to a much greater visibility of the positive impacts of their actions that extend to other areas of daily life. In addition, the community brought these benefits into alignment, thus suggesting that environmental health and economic benefits go hand in hand. This is in stark contrast to discourses currently circulating in the British media in which the delay of climate-positive actions by the government are presented as providing economic relief for low-income families (Martin, Oliver and Brignal 2023). In other words, a community-led approach to reporting (Malik et al. 2019) on environmentally positive actions develops a much more complex, and most of all much more positive, representation of what climate action can involve.

Local climate action and hope

We followed up the screening of these programmes with a qualitative questionnaire to get a sense of what impact programmes such as the one about Aigburth Community Cycle Club might have on the community. It was noticeable that the screenings were met with widespread positivity. Many respondents emphasised the positive energy they felt could be vicariously experienced through watching the programmes. Thus, in a moment when we may fear the effects of climate change, programmes about community projects fill audiences with hope. More important, however, was that they inspired those currently not involved in any of these groups. As one respondent wrote: '[the programmes were] great for communicating what is going on in [the] local area and how we can get involved'. Thus, the current lack of reporting of such community efforts makes it harder for those who don't know what to do to become involved. Importantly, reporting needs to be specific to the localities of the residents; otherwise, climate action, like climate change, appears as something that is done 'over there', that is, it is spatially distant from viewers (Braasch 2013). But climate action happens everywhere, and it is precisely by showcasing 'the little things you do [that] can have a massive impact' as another respondent put it, that removes the sense of being overwhelmed that eco-anxiety and existential dread can engender.

In other words, the reporting of climate change as disasters needs to be balanced with stories of local communities already doing their bit. As our community-led approach shows, local communities are already doing a lot, and they are very good at articulating the variety of benefits to their actions, including those not directly linked to the environment. It is by representing both the co-benefits of climate action and 'the little things' that people can do, that others, who are currently not doing a lot, can be inspired.

Acknowledgement

This chapter is an outcome of the British Academy funded project 'Community-led Television, Local Voice and Climate Action', funded through their Shared Understandings of Sustainable Futures stream. Reference: Application SSF\210053

References

Gary Braasch (2013) 'Climate change: is seeing believing?' *Bulletin of the Atomic Scientists*, Vol. 69, No. 6 pp. 33–41

Countryfile (1988-present) Bristol: BBC Studios Factual Entertainment Productions.

Gardeners' World (1968-present) Herefordshire: BBC Studios Factual Entertainment Productions.

Alexandre Heeren, Camille Mouguiama-Daouda, and Alba Contreras (2022) 'On Climate Anxiety and the Threat It May Pose to Daily Life Functioning and Adaptation: A Study among European and African French-Speaking Participants', *Climatic Change: An Interdisciplinary, International Journal Devoted to the Description, Causes and Implications of Climatic Change*, Vol. 173, No. 15.

Matteo Innocenti, Gabriele Santarelli, Gaia Surya Lombardi, Lorenzo Ciabini, Doris Zjalic, Mattia Di Russo, and Chiara Cadeddu (2023) 'How Can Climate Change Anxiety Induce Both Pro-Environmental Behaviours and Eco-Paralysis? The Mediating Role of General Self Efficacy,' *International Journal of Environmental Research and Public Health* Vol. 20, No.3085.

Sarita Malik, Caroline Chapain, and Roberta Comunian (eds) (2019) *Community Filmmaking: Diversity, Practices and Places*, Routledge Studies in Media and Cultural Industries, 1. London: Routledge.

Daniel Martin, Matt Oliver, and Mattie Brignal (2023) 'How Rishi Sunak watering down his net zero pledges will help consumers', *The Telegraph*, 20 September.

Joseph T.C. Rehling (2022) 'Conceptualising Eco-Anxiety Using an Existential Framework,' *South African Journal of Psychology*, Vol. 52, No. 4 pp. 472–485.

George Ritzer and Nathan Jurgenson (2010) 'Production, Consumption, Prosumption: The Nature of Capitalism in the Age of the Digital "prosumer",' *Journal of Consumer Culture*, Vol. 10, No. 1 pp. 13–36.

Douglas A. Vakoch and Sam Mickey (eds) (2022) *Eco-anxiety and Planetary Hope: Experiencing the Twin Disasters of Covid-19 and Climate Change*, Cham: Springer.

Lorraine Whitmarsh, Lois Player, Angelica Jiongco, Melissa James, Marc Williams, Elizabeth Marks and Patrick Kennedy-Williams (2022) 'Climate Anxiety: What Predicts It and How Is It Related to Climate Action?' *Journal of Environmental Psychology*, Vol. 83.

YouGov (2023). 'The Most Important Issues Facing the Country', YouGov, <https://yougov.co.uk/topics/society/trackers/the-most-important-issues-facing-the-country> (Accessed 18 September)

About the contributors

Dr Elke Weissmann is Reader in Film and Television at Edge Hill University. She has published widely on television, in particular on *Transnational Television Drama* (2012). She is also editor of *Critical Studies in Television*, and head of Edge Hill University's Television Studies Research Group. Belinda Tyrrell is a research associate at the University of Liverpool's Heseltine Institute. A former policy and programmes officer at Liverpool City Council, Belinda worked on the performance monitoring of externally funded programmes including Neighbourhood Renewal Fund, and Housing Market Renewal Initiative, and was part of the Project Liverpool Team which mapped and tracked the value of Area Based Initiatives within the City of Liverpool.

Chapter 12

The range and depth of BBC News and Current Affairs: a climate change case study

In this edited extract from a substantial report Cardiff University's **Stephen Cushion** examines news coverage of climate change over three weeks in June 2019

As the news ecology has transformed over recent years, connecting with audiences and raising public understanding of complex issues have become more challenging journalistic goals. The ways in which people consume and engage with media is in flux as more people turn to new online and social media platforms for news and information. Broadcasting is no longer the monopoly news provider as media consumption becomes a more fluid and fragmented experience. Moreover, in the digital age the number of television and radio channels has increased, giving people an unprecedented choice of information sources.

Given this increasingly crowded and competitive media marketplace, concerns have understandably been raised about the range and depth of programming available in today's news ecology. The BBC – the UK's main public service broadcaster – is often the focus of these concerns, not just because its journalism is funded by a public licence fee, but because it is, according to Ofcom, 'expected to provide high-quality, creative content that is distinctive across all its output and services; and that includes news and current affairs across all platforms'.

By conducting a systematic content analysis of BBC and commercial news and current affairs across TV, radio and online in a three-week period of June 2019, our project was designed to provide an evidence-based assessment of the range and depth of journalism across different platforms and news providers. The full report offers case studies of BBC coverage of the 2019 Conservative leadership contest, Brexit, health and education in a devolved UK, and climate change. This chapter is a summary of the climate change case study.

The UK government and climate change

Across all the outlets covered in the three-week study, climate change made up a very small percentage of total news coverage. There were some major stories in the sample period, notably the Conservative leadership contest, which dominated the news agenda and may have influenced the level of news about the environment. However, the issue of climate change did become a prominent topic on one day of the sample period, when the government announced a net zero emissions target on 12 June 2019.

In this case study, we compared how different news providers reported this announcement. In doing so, we examined the depth of policy information provided by news providers, the range of sources used to inform coverage, and the degree to which the government's claims were appropriately challenged by journalists.

Level of policy information and framing of government announcement

Broadly speaking, we found that outlets provided either some policy context or a more detailed level of information about the government's plan.

All outlets provided a general sense of how the government would deliver the net zero target by 2050 and pointed out that people need to eat less meat and dairy, switch to electric cars and take fewer flights in order for the emissions reduction to be achieved. All commercial radio outlets, in this respect, provided some degree of policy information in their items about this story but this was largely limited to repeating the government's announcement to reduce emissions to net zero.

The BBC *World at One* reported one item about the government's plans to counter climate change, framing the story as the UK being the first country to legislate for the target and it being widely supported, while also referring to critical voices, including those who say the pledge is 'impossible' to achieve.

All television and BBC radio outlets provided relatively detailed information about the government's plans to cut emissions to zero, but there were differences in the selection of sources and how critical they were towards the proposal.

The BBC *News at Ten*, for example, introduced the government's plans, referencing widespread support by campaigners, while also acknowledging critics who say that it is either too late to have any meaningful impact or that it is an 'impossible task' to counter climate change.

ITV *News at Ten*, which was the only bulletin to make the climate change policy its lead story, introduced the item by stating that tackling climate change had generally been slow but this had been enhanced by the government's 'ambitious plans'. In the follow up item, the anchor provided some useful context and background to the challenge of cutting emissions so drastically.

On *Channel 4 News*, where the topic was much further down the news agenda, the government's plan was outlined and broadly praised by campaigners, but there were no critical voices in the introduction to the package.

Finally, Channel 5 personalised coverage by referencing the Prime Minister's political situation and referred to the announcement as 'a bold pledge', without acknowledging critical voices about the government's target:

Similarly, Radio 5 Live *Breakfast* outlined May's target to cut emissions, drawing on a source from the energy industry who reinforced the government's message and did not include any critical opposition to the plan. *Newsbeat*, in contrast, offered a more conversational style than other news providers in its reporting, focusing on personalities to help frame the news on the emissions target.

The way the story was framed in the opening headlines on Radio 4's *Today* was similar to how *World at One* had introduced the government announcement. The report by Roger Harrabin was a longer and more detailed version than was featured on *World at One*. The Today programme returned to the topic later with a lengthy studio discussion and interviews.

Overall, in their initial framing of the government's announcement, BBC outlets tended to adopt a more critical stance than commercial media.

Reporting the urgency of meeting the 2050 net zero emissions target

Given the urgency of reducing emissions, which scientists have long called for, we considered how much this was stressed by journalists in each news item. In doing so, we broadly observed whether the coverage made *no* substantive reference to the urgency of reducing the emissions target, if there was *some* reference to it, or if the urgency was clearly communicated.

Commercial radio items did not stress any real urgency about enacting the government's plan, partly – as already acknowledged – because of the limited time they had to communicate news. Across BBC radio items, there were several items where no real urgency was communicated. For example, while the *World at One* referenced the government's message that the UK was the first 'major nation' to cut carbon emissions to almost zero, the only mention of urgency came in the anchor's introduction, when it was briefly stated:

'Some critics say the phase-out is too late to protect the climate.'

When the urgency of meeting the 2050 net zero target was communicated, it tended to be through the use of external sources, rather than by the journalists. On the BBC News Channel, *Newsbeat*, Radio 4, ITV, and *Channel 5 News*, each outlet included an item where there was some reference to the urgency of meeting the target, but this was not unequivocal.

By going beyond the government's announcement, and drawing on the UN Climate Panel report, the need for an immediate reduction in emissions was more clearly communicated on the BBC *News at Ten* than on other outlets. Channel 4 News drew attention to the contradiction between the urgent calls by climate change campaigners and the thirty-year span of the target, as well as other proposed policies.

Which sources informed coverage; and were the government's claims challenged?

In terms of political sources, BBC Radio 5 Live *Breakfast* was the only outlet to interview a government minister - Chris Skidmore, the Interim Energy and Clean Growth Minister. BBC 4 *Today* interviewed Ed Miliband, Labour opposition MP and former Environment and Climate Change Minister. Other outlets used edited clips from film and radio interviews, or statements by Theresa May, the Prime Minister, and Caroline Lucas, Green MP.

With the exception of the BBC News Channel and Radio 4's *World at One*, all the BBC items featured a government source. But these perspectives, in most cases, were counterbalanced by critical voices from climate change charities and campaigners or opposition MPs. There were also sources drawn from international bodies such as the UN, academics, an energy group and science charities. ITV *News at Ten*, *Channel 4 News* and *Channel 5 News* constructed a similar balance of information sources. Channel 4 and Channel 5, however, featured experts who considered the future of sustainable housing.

On BBC radio, there was a similar balance between a government source and climate charities and campaigners, along with experts in energy. Radio 4 featured a lengthy interview involving an academic and the former Secretary of State for Climate Change and Energy, Ed Miliband, which included a broader discussion about the historical challenges of meeting emissions targets and the contemporary international context.

Overall, with the exception of talkRADIO and some follow-up items, all outlets included sources critical of the government's plans. However, on Channel 5 and ITV News. some of these critical sources provided mixed responses; they were supportive while raising issues with the government's target. On all the BBC outlets government perspectives were counterbalanced by critical voices.

To what degree was the government's plan scrutinised?

In almost all the items, news providers mainly focused on reporting the government's general claim to reach net zero emissions by 2050. In doing so, the different outlets drew heavily on a range of government claims from sources other than just the Prime Minister.

With the exception of Heart and Channel 5, all news providers challenged the government's claims, either directly by a journalist or by referring to a direct or indirect source. There were only a few items that did not include a challenge to a government claim, but these were follow-up items where a government representative may not have been directly involved in the coverage, such as the interview with an academic and a former Secretary of State for Energy and Climate Change.

Within the reporter packages across the outlets, it was mainly left to sources, either directly or indirectly, to challenge the government plans, rather than journalists. Climate campaigners, opposition MPs, academics and housing groups were featured, raising concerns that the policy was not strategically broad enough, or urgent enough, to achieve the targets. In the commercial TV and BBC radio interviews journalists, through their questioning, directly challenged the government's policy and the likelihood of meeting its target.

Across several BBC outlets (but not in the commercial coverage) there was criticism of the government's 2050 target because it allowed the government to offset its carbon footprint by relying on imported goods that had been produced in a high-emissions country. For example, Deiter Helm, a British economist and academic, was interviewed on BBC News Online, BBC *News at Ten*, and *Today*.

While all reporter packages across the outlets gave an overview of the government's policy, they varied in depth of challenge, analysis, and context. Channel 5 provided a brief overview of the government's announcement before going into more depth about one of the major changes needed to achieve the policy. Along with *Channel 4 News*, the BBC News channel and BBC *News at Ten*, *Channel 5 News* at 5pm went to a site of new low-emission buildings and interviewed sources about the emissions target and the changes needed.

Taken together, our analysis showed that BBC outlets were generally more critical than commercial media of the government's climate change policy, challenging rather than accepting its plan to meet the emissions target.

This chapter is an edited extract from Cardiff University's 'The range and depth of BBC News and Current Affairs: a content analysis', 2019.

About the contributor

Professor Stephen Cushion is Director of Research Development and Environment at Cardiff University's School of Journalism, Media, and Culture. The production of his 2019 Ofcom commissioned report was supported by the research team of Marina Morani, Jason Roberts, Andy Nelmes, Arron Cullen, Lizzy Willmington, and Claire Thurlow.

Chapter 13

Is Fleet Street still in climate change denial?

Three years after her initial survey of UK newspaper climate change coverage **Liz Gerard** returned to see if anything had changed

Well, it didn't look that way on Monday 24 July 2023. In common with other Tory-leaning papers, *The Times* was focused on Sunak's reported retreat from what he believes to be unpopular eco policies. In this he was spurred on by the Tory by-election win in Uxbridge, which was put down to the planned extension of London's ultra-low emissions zone (Ulez) to encompass Boris Johnson's old constituency.

Ulez was introduced by Johnson himself when mayor and the expansion was indirectly endorsed by the government in 2021, when transport secretary Grant Shapps told Sadiq Khan that, if he retreated on that policy, he should expect no help from Whitehall to make up the income shortfall.

Be that as it may, the Uxbridge victory was seen by the climate-sceptic Press as proof that eco-friendly policies (like the eco-maniacs and eco-warriors and eco-mob) were unpopular and gave them the green light (oops!) to push for further watering down.

That this should all take centre stage against a backdrop of the wildfires in Greece was unfortunate, to put it mildly. For the previous two weeks, the foreign pages had been reporting on the heatwave in southern Europe. Then the fires broke out in Rhodes. Then the British press woke up to the fact that this was the first week of the school holidays and quite a lot of Brits go to Rhodes for their summer break.

On Monday 24 July 2023, the *Express* splash was 'Hell on earth – Brits flee raging fires on Rhodes', the *Mirror* had 'Our terror' and 'Rhodes inferno agony', the *Telegraph*, 'Pressure on travel firms to fly Britons out of Rhodes', and the *Sun*, 'Run for your lives'. It was only natural that the focus would be on British holidaymakers and the evacuation (I loved the person on Twitter who noted that the first thought of Greeks faced with Brits fleeing on small boats was to offer the women and children food, comfort, and shelter). But where was the background to this? Where was mention of the searing heatwave of the previous days, not only in Europe but across the world? Any explanation of the cause of the wildfires?

And the *Times*? It went for the juxtaposition to end all juxtapositions. A photograph of holidaymakers walking away from a ball of flame and smoke with a headline about the scramble to leave Rhodes alongside a splash saying, 'Tory retreat from green policies to woo voters'. Inside, the top leader, headlined 'Apocalypse Not' asserted that it was an open question whether the fires in Rhodes were directly attributable to global warming. It conceded that climate change was a serious danger, and even that 'human activities' were responsible for the increase in carbon in the atmosphere, but there had to be a trade-off in how to tackle it. Somehow we had to manage climate change without giving up the good things in life.

THE TIMES

My big fat middle-aged wedding

The £99 DNA test that tells you what to eat

Spanish PM could gain seats but lose power after snap election

Tory retreat from green policies to woo voters

'Aston Martin exemption' for petrol ban on cards

Airlines lead scramble to help 19,000 flee Rhodes

And remember, heat-related deaths in Spain have fallen since the 1980s and cold is more lethal than heat for the vulnerable in Britain. This is the sort of accurate, rather than incendiary, reporting that the leader advocates. Sounds a bit simplistic to me. Maybe they have better air conditioning in Spain these days?

The threat to the planet isn't the effect on individuals in particular countries of a degree or so on the average temperature, it's about weather extremes, both hot and cold, melting snowcaps, rising sea levels, floods, storms, dangers to wildlife, an upset in the balance of nature, island nations disappearing under water and much more. But the *Times* knows that. And so do we all.

So, I raise my glass to the *i* for the better headline that day: ‘Tories warned over fiddling with green policies . . . whole Rhodes burns’. A heading that not only captured the basic facts of the events that day, but also neatly encapsulated the essence behind them with its wordplay. One of those headlines that is glaringly obvious – once someone else has written it.

Meanwhile, if *Times* leader writers are still doubtful whether the Greek fires can be put down to global warming, perhaps they might like to read Tuesday 25 July 2023’s *Guardian*: ‘Climate crisis link to heatwave fires undeniable, say scientists’.

Section:GDN 1N PaGe:1 Edition Date:230725 Edition:01 Zone:S Sent at 24/7/2023 21:22

How to garden on a budget
Can you dig it?
G2

George Alagiah Tributes as BBC journalist dies aged 67
News

Tuesday 25 July 2023
£2.80
From £2.13 for subscribers

The Guardian
Newspaper of the year

Climate crisis link to heatwave fires undeniable, say scientists

- Analysis shows human-caused global temperature rises to blame for destruction
- Warning to cut emissions fast comes as Sunak faces calls to axe green policies

Damian Carrington
Environment editor

The human-caused climate crisis is undeniably to blame for the deadly heatwaves that have struck Europe and the United States in recent weeks, scientists have shown.

Both would have been virtually impossible without global heating driven by burning fossil fuels, new analysis shows. Another heatwave, in China, was made 50 times more likely by the climate crisis.

The results make it crystal clear that human-caused global heating is destroying lives and livelihoods across the world, making the need to cut emissions ever more urgent. Such brutal heatwaves were no longer rare today, the scientists said, and would worsen as emissions continued to rise. If the world heats by 2C, they will happen every two to five years.

A report by climate scientists in March, endorsed by the world's governments, said: "There is a rapidly closing window of opportunity to secure a liveable and sustainable future for all."

The analysis demonstrated how rapidly that window is closing.

In recent days Downing Street has suggested it could delay or abandon certain green policies – a move that would enrage environmental groups who believe this is a moment to move faster, not slower, in the face of the climate emergency.

Under pressure from some MPs and the rightwing press after last week's Uxbridge and Ruislip byelection – in which the Conservative candidate squeaked home by campaigning against the expansion of London's ultra-low emission zone (Ulez) – No 10 said yesterday that it would "continually examine and scrutinise" its green policies. Rishi Sunak said he

▲ *Firefighters, volunteers and police officers battle a wildfire near the village of Asklipieio on Rhodes*

▲ *Rishi Sunak faces pressure to row back on environmental policies*

Or the *Mirror* from the previous week – before all the 'Brits in holiday terror' jingoism. This focused on the real issue with a stark cover headlined 'BURNING UP'. This was the 'heatwave from hell', illustrated by 'a child carried from their blazing home as inferno temperatures sweep across Europe'. This, the paper, said was the 'terrifying reality of today's climate crisis'.

DAILY Mirror

Newspaper of the Year

FREE £2 SHOP BET WITH William HILL

FREE INSIDE: WOMEN'S WORLD CUP PULLOUT

HEATWAVE FROM HELL

A child is carried from their blazing home as inferno temperatures sweep across Europe. This is the terrifying reality of today's climate crisis...

BURNING UP

Quite so. But much of the press and many MPs remain in denial, urging the Government to abandon or shelve net zero measures and green taxes. In September, the *Times* was again splashing on pressure for a delay in the ban on new petrol and diesel cars. This time, though, Rishi Sunak – the man who had just approved a hundred new oil drilling licences in the North Sea –

was reportedly insistent that the 2030 target date would not be put back.

Because it would harm the planet? No. Because it would be 'damaging to industry'. Britain is negotiating with BMW to build electric Minis in Oxford rather than China. If petrol cars were reprieved, the deal might fall through.

Did *The Times* get it wrong or did Sunak waver? For two days later the BBC was leading on a leak that not only would petrol and diesel cars be given a five-year reprieve, but that a whole raft of other on-the-way-to-net-zero targets were being junked. With Parliament conveniently in recess, the PM duly made his announcement from the media room at No 9, promising also to 'stop' a series of policies, such as requiring families to separate rubbish into seven bins, that no one had ever started. The Press response? The *Times* reported it straight, like a cat pretending it didn't just fall from a shelf, ignoring the fact that the news was the direct reverse of what it had told readers the previous Saturday. The *Mail*, *Express*, *Sun*, and *Telegraph* were delighted with 'honest Rishi' who had 'given us a brake' and spared people the 'ruinous cost' of net zero plans.

And the *Mirror*? It splashed on veterans who had been involved in nuclear tests 70 years ago starting a legal fight to gain access to their medical records. A good exclusive story that was the result of persistent digging by the paper. But did it have to run that day? Sunak's retreat was on pages 8 and 9 under the heading 'Fossil fool'.

That narrow Uxbridge by-election win seems to have created a received wisdom that green policies are not only unpopular, but that the fate of the planet is subservient to the particular interests of small groups of elderly people – whether they are drivers of old cars or victims of an MoD cover-up.

Tackling climate change is the number one issue for younger generations. But it's the older generations who vote and buy newspapers. So it's on with the blinkers for right-wing politicians and press. Fire up the gas boiler, fill the tank with diesel and be merry, for tomorrow we die. And if the planet does too? We won't be there to worry. Let the kids deal with it.

This chapter is an edited and updated version of part of Liz Gerard's 27 July 2023 *InPublishing* column.

SECTION FOUR

Front Lines: LTNS and Ulez

Introduction

John Mair

It is on the streets that the battle for hearts and minds on climate change is being fought, especially the London streets. LTNs (Low Traffic Neighbourhoods) and Ulez (Ultra Low Emission Zones) are the Alsace-Lorraine of these culture wars. The battles are intense with Ulez cameras being vandalized by (Conservative, sometimes) activists and bollards in LTNs being ripped up. Beyond paper arguments, there is now physical, often illegal, action.

And it's not just London either. I live in Oxford and the front line here is in East Oxford where largely British Pakistani taxi drivers deprived of rat runs and easy access to the Mosque are pitted against posh, university-educated liberals who want quiet streets. That battle front is daily and dirty,

In this section, we analyse those arguments on paper.

First off is Raymond Snoddy, former media editor of the *Times*. In 'The way to the nation's vote' he traces the September 2023 Damascene conversion of Prime Minister Rishi Sunak to the seminal (in his view) Uxbridge and South Ruislip by election in July 2023.That was won on an Anti-Ulez platform. Egged on by the Conservative-supporting national papers - *The Mail, Express, Telegraph* - the PM did what journalists call a reverse ferret on key net zero measures, especially the 2030 compulsory introduction of Electric vehicles (EVs). From (reluctant) climate change acceptors the newspapers became megaphones for rowing back. They were pro-motorist, pro car, the modern symbol of freedom so good it was sui generis. All caution was thrown to the wind: 'There was no mention that by watering down its climate change action, at least for now, it might be encouraging others around the world to do something similar. Is there also a danger that going easy now might backload even larger costs later, quite apart from creating increased uncertainty for manufacturers? [...] Totally absent from the coverage was any mention of the disconnect between delaying climate targets and the regular reports of death and mayhem from floods and forest fires, or warnings from climate scientists that it's already almost too late for the survival of normal life on our planet'.

The debate about LTNS can become equally toxic and heated. Maggie Brown is a fellow distinguished retired media correspondent, in her case for *The Independent* and the *Observer*. But when and LTN came calling to her Dulwich South London home impartiality left her. In 'One LTN, one woman, and . . . misery!' she rails against Southwark Council policy and, she says, the havoc, it has wreaked on her and neighbours' lives. She gets close to saying it has ruined her four-decade idyll. She is coruscating: 'LTN policy is a lesson in how not to do climate change policy, by dividing communities with blatantly obvious discrimination, resulting "In millionaires sitting like Roman Emperors being served by a Labour council," a resident tartly told Catherine Rose, the cabinet minister at Southwark for Parks, Streets, and Clean Air. [...] Those informed on local council regulation believe they are 'overstepping the mark' into ultra vires territory, dictating social policy by imposing lifestyle changes while raising millions in extra revenue from fines and hiked parking dues, for diversion into what: subsidising a Southwark levelling up policy?'

A fellow journalist of some distinction, Christian Wolmar who commands the transport, especially trains, field of the craft, is of a diametrically opposed view. In 'LTNs: one man, another view, less misery' he confronts Maggie Brown head on: 'The LTNs which Maggie complains about are part of this wider jigsaw which, when pieced together, is about taming the car. It is not anti-motorist but pro-people. Of course, sometimes schemes are misconceived or don't work out as planned. Some main roads may get an increase in traffic but the name is on the tin – 'main'. That's what they are designed for. […] Therefore LTNs, by reducing through running in some streets – they never block off housing totally unlike what some antis claim – nudge some people into looking at alternatives. Residential roads need to be protected from through running which is not their purpose. Just look at the pictures of these streets from the days before the dominance of motorisation and there are kids playing, neighbours chatting and a sense of tranquillity'.

Two tribes going to war on the streets of London, Oxford, Cambridge, and Newcastle.

There is an alternative intellectual view. Philip Hammond is emeritus professor of Media and Communications. One would expect him to be in the

Christian Wolmar/London Mayor Sadiq Khan, pro Ulez camp. He is not. In 'The Ulez front in the climate culture' war he positions himself firmly on the side of the disruptors of the new status quo: 'A democratic deficit, rather than a culture clash, is at the heart of the conflict over Ulez and other climate policies. Britain's Net Zero policy, adopted in 2019, was not part of any political programme or manifesto offered to the public, for example. Rather, it emerged from an unaccountable quango, the Committee on Climate Change, and passed into law in a matter of weeks. Whatever one thinks of the policy, Britain's Net Zero law clearly bypassed the sorts of democratic decision-making processes that would normally be expected to precede a government passing legislation with such far-reaching implications. [...] In this context, characterising disagreement over environmental policies such as Ulez as a culture war waged by extremists is not a description so much as an attempt to quash dissent'.

Such sensible debate is or should be at the heart of all discussions of climate measures in action. It is not. Irrationality rules. Many of the arguments made against the EC, Covid restrictions, the Davos elite are now transferred lock stock and smoking cameras to EVs, LTNs, and Ulez. No conspiracy goes unreported in this age of social media. Keyboard warriors in back rooms have the floor. They are either the clarion callers of democracy or the sewer of modern Britain.

But the MSM (Mainstream Media), the printed press, despite falling sales, still matters. They form or inform opinions. Jon Fuller is an obsessive about newspapers.

He reads them avidly, and cuts them every day for a weekly report to his followers. We gave him the task of analysing one week of British nationals one week in late September 2023, the week of the Rishi Sunak reverse ferret and the Rosebank oil announcement. He was not impressed with their Climate coverage. In 'The lies they tell' he calls them out for stereotyping activists and neglecting the bigger picture: 'Right-wing papers have long hurled abuse at climate protesters, with the term 'eco-extremist' and 'eco-clowns' used in connection with a Just Stop Oil protest in the week. The *Daily Star* has a unique twist on this, referring to all climate protesters as 'Tarquin', in an attempt to portray climate activists as upper-class toffs. But the papers don't leave the abuse there. In an attempt to undermine efforts to decarbonising, they even abuse people who support the 2050 target as 'eco-zealots' or 'eco fanatics', with *The Sun's* Trevor Kavanagh (25 September) calling the attempt to reach net-zero as a 'green cult'. […] In the absence of responsible reporting, it is left to groups such as XR (Extinction Rebellion) to focus significant effort on the media in the attempt to get them to tell the whole truth. In my view, it is the single most important part of our endeavour to save all life on Earth'.

Read on. We hope a flavour of the bush fires on the frontlines of the climate change war will come through the smoke on these pages. Who will win and who will lose? Probably the planet and the lives of our children and grandchildren.

About the contributor

John Mair is co-editor of *Toxic News*.

Chapter 14

The way to the nation's vote

Raymond Snoddy examines how Rishi Sunak, the 'motorist's friend' is helped by the Tory press in delaying climate change measures

The outline of the UK government's general election campaign is becoming crystal clear, amplified and encouraged almost daily in the Conservative supporting newspapers.

Home Secretary Suella Braverman revealed that one line of attack will be trying to clamp down on refugees, even to the extent of threatening to leave or modify the UN Convention on Refugees, and on the most visible manifestation of asylum seekers, the small boats. Another line of attack will be an attempt to portray Labour leader Sir Keir Starmer as being 'soft on Brexit', and likely to betray Brexit because of his insistence that the UK should work more closely with the European Union.

The central plank of Prime Minister Rishi Sunak's line of attack, however, is likely to be embracing motorists in all shapes and sizes and turning his back on major rail infrastructure projects by axing the HS2 link from Birmingham to Manchester. The pro-motorist package looks like placing limits on 20mph zones and, much more significantly, easing the time pressure on motorists to go all-electric while at the same time, insisting, rather implausibly, that the net zero target of 2050 has not been changed.

Pouring oil on the climate fire

In the arena of climate change there was the huge decision to allow the enormous Rosebank oil and gas field west of the Shetland Islands to go ahead. The field is estimated to produce around 300 million barrels of oil.

It is the twin decisions to row back on the timetable of steps on the way to net zero and the go-ahead for Rosefield that best exemplify Sunak's approach to taking meaningful measures to tackle climate change. They also demonstrate the symbiotic relationship between Sunak, and indeed the four previous Prime Ministers of varying quality, and the Conservative-supporting newspapers, and the tabloids in particular.

The Tories and the press - bound together

Newspapers such as *The Sun, the Daily Mail*, and *the Daily Express,* while recognising that climate change is real and that something must be done became cheerleaders in trying to ensure that 'something' appears neither effective, pressing, nor radical.

As with their instinctive scepticism about Covid, lockdowns, and working from home, their approach to climate change is a short-term one, which places the emphasis on the immediate health of the economy, combined with trying to win another term in office for the Conservatives.

Unusually for the emergence of policies, the present emphasis on being the motorist's friend and delaying some of the measures designed to mitigate climate can be identified with a particular event and a specific day.

The day that changed the Tory world

The origins of the new strand of Conservative thinking that just might provide a path to general election victory came on 20 July 2023.

Three by-elections were held on that day and the Conservatives themselves expected to lose all three heavily. That was very nearly what happened. In South West England the safe Conservative seat of Somerset and Frome fell to the Liberal Democrats, and in the North of England the Conservative seat of Selby and Ainsty was won by Labour. The same was supposed to happen to Boris Johnson's old seat in West London, Uxbridge.

Instead, against all the apparent odds, while the 7,000 Conservative majority there all but evaporated, the party managed to hang on by 495 votes.

It was quickly identified that the principal factor behind the upset was opposition to the extension of the Ultra Low Emission Zones (Ulez) to Greater London, including Uxbridge. Never mind that Ulez was originally a Conservative policy in London, that narrow hold gave party strategists something to get their teeth into.

Its development can most clearly be seen in the delays to the switchover from petrol and diesel cars to electric, in the go-ahead for the licensing of the Rosebank field, and in the reaction of the Conservative-supporting national newspapers to both decisions.

Push back on EVs

Prime Minister Sunak announced on 20 September that he was pushing back the ban on the sale of new petrol and diesel cars from 2030 to 2035. There would also be 5m permanent exemptions from the forthcoming oil and gas domestic boiler ban, and increased grants for those having to install heat pumps.

There was enthusiastic and largely uncritical support for the Prime Minister's move in the ranks of the Conservative press. As the splash headline in the *Daily Mail* on 21 September put it: "I'll Spare Families Ruinous Cost of Net Zero, Vows Rishi".

The change was portrayed as Sunak 'hitting the brakes on the race to net zero', although well down the story there was a comment from Sir Alok Sharma, Conservative president of the COP26, climate summit expressing doubt that any political party would gain electorally from such a decision. Former Prime Minister Boris Johnson commented that Britain could not afford to falter now 'or in any way lose our ambition for this country'.

The Johnson approach was not reflected in the *Daily Mail* comment section where it was of course acknowledged that the world needed to change to counter global warning. But Prime Minister Sunak should be congratulated 'for injecting a badly needed dose of common sense into the climate change programme', the paper said.

The policy change was hailed as 'a stunning victory' for the *Mail*'s Rethink The Petrol Car Ban campaign.

It was also rather convenient politically that the policy set down a demarcation line - a wedge - between the Conservatives and Labour. Rather oddly the *Mail* Comment concluded: 'That's the difference between the two parties. Labour's leader is looking out for his own interests. Mr Sunak is taking tough decisions to benefit the whole nation.'

Is it the *Sun* wot won it?

The *Sun* too had been campaigning, and indeed the Prime Minster hailed the paper's 'Give Us a Brake' campaign.

Sunak even had a piece in the paper vowing he would not punish *Sun* readers to get to net zero. In its comment column the *Sun* argued that Rishi Sunak had rightly braved the flak to put families' finances and their standard of living before what it called eco dogma. 'We salute him,' the *Sun* concluded.

The *Daily Express* said the PM had pushed back green policies that hard-up voters cannot afford in the cost-of-living crisis. The *Daily Telegraph* chose to highlight that fact that Sir Jacob Rees-Mogg had claimed on the controversial TV channel GB News that the changes to net zero policy could help the Conservatives to win the next election.

Even *The Times* leader page came out firmly for Sunak and said he deserved credit for 'grasping the green nettle'. The Prime Minister had confronted 'a truth politicians of all parties have neglected in favour of faddish radicalism: to lumber working people with the cost of net zero is to undermine the public consent that is so vital for consensus on the environment'.

It is unclear what climate scientists would make of the 'faddish radicalism' tag.

None of the newspapers saw any contradiction in the Prime Minister's position that, despite putting 'the brakes on' the move to all electric vehicles and ending gas boiler installation, somehow the original net zero target of 2050 could be met.

Omissions?

There was no mention that by watering down its climate change action, at least for now, it might be encouraging others around the world to do something similar. Is there also a danger that going easy now might backload even larger costs later, quite apart from creating increased uncertainty for manufacturers?

Totally absent from the coverage was any mention of the disconnect between delaying climate targets and the regular reports of death and mayhem from floods and forest fires, or warnings from climate scientists that it's already almost too late for the survival of normal life on our planet.

Banking on Rosebank; Norway gains

Then a week later there came the decision to go ahead with the last great untapped reserve of oil and gas in the North Sea, a move enthusiastically received by the Conservative-supporting press. According to *The Times* the Government was right to license the new oilfield off Shetland although there was the caveat that safeguarding Britain's energy supply should not compromise progress towards a low carbon future.

Again, the appearance of a disconnect.

The front pages that day, 28 September 2023, were understandably dominated by the brutal murder of 15-year-old Croydon schoolgirl Elianne Andam. But plenty of space was devoted to Rosebank, which they argued had had rightly received a government licence.

'We need to extract our own oil and gas a cleanly as possible - without having to beg for it from abroad,' the *Sun* said. The *Daily Mail* approach was to argue that the need for fossil fuels couldn't be wished away and that, in the age of Putin, anything that made our energy stocks more secure was welcome.

Those who criticised the decision, such as environmental campaigner Chris Packham and the Green Party, were denounced as producing 'a predictable outpouring of hysteria'.

Never mind the environment, little emphasis was given to the business details of the deal - the £3.75 billion in tax breaks or that the oil will be extracted by a Norwegian-led consortium, and landed and refined in Norway. The finished product will then be priced and sold in the international market and will have little impact on increasing the UK's energy security.

By chance two other ironies could be seen in that day's newspapers. One was an alarming report detailing how one in five British species had declined over the past 50 years – and that environmental loss and climate change were involved.

The Civitas 'truth'

Perhaps even more telling was the way national newspapers, including *the Sun, the Times, the Daily*

Mail, and the *Daily Express* happily covered a report from the right-wing think tank Civitas, based at the (increasingly notorious) London address 55 Tufton Street. It claimed that the path to net zero would cost every household £6,000 every year to 2050.It was written by climate sceptic Ewen Stewart, who is 2021 described human-caused global warming as 'a contested theory'.

As *The Guardian* pointed out, the report was riddled with schoolboy errors including ignoring any savings achieved along the way to net zero. According to the *Guardian* Stewart confused power capacity in megawatts (MW) with electricity generation in megawatt hours (MWh). As a result, Civitas produced a cost for onshore wind power that was 10,000 times higher than the reality and 'then compounded his embarrassment by mixing up billions with trillions'. Nevertheless, that claim appeared in four national newspapers.

On the main battlefronts, such as putting the brakes on the path to net zero and licensing new oil fields, critics say that the Prime Minister is hoping such policies, born after the Uxbridge byelection, will deflect from the cost-of-living crisis, the state of the NHS, and the embarrassment of sewage in rivers and on beaches across the country.

About the contributor

Raymond Snoddy OBE is the former media editor of *The Times* and the *Financial Times*. His publications include: *The Good, the Bad and the Unacceptable:*

the Hard News about the British Press (Faber & Faber 1993), *Greenfinger: the rise of Michael Green and Carlton Communications* (Faber & Faber 1996), and *It Could Be You: the Untold Story of the National Lottery* (Faber & Faber 2001). He is now a freelance writer.

Chapter 15

One LTN, one woman, and . . . misery!

Do Low Traffic Neighbourhoods (LTNs) suit everybody? Or are they imposed without consultation and just bring chaos to neighbouring streets? **Maggie Brown** thinks the latter

In August 2020 we returned to our Dulwich house of 37 years to find ourselves on a mini version of the South Circular, with the added affliction of surveillance cameras poised to fine drivers if they put a wheel wrong.

In a rapid summer coup, with effect from January 2021, Southwark Council had imposed a confusing mix of Low Traffic Neighbourhood blocked roads and timed traffic closures, six hours a day, where motorists who disobeyed were to be slapped with a £65 penalty.

We now lived on a 'boundary' road, whose role was to take displaced traffic from favoured LTNs. The instant effect then and now was far greater congestion rather than obediently 'evaporating' traffic plus extra pollution.

As my husband and I walked around in disbelief, for we had not been consulted, we spotted our local Labour councillor at the crossroads of Dulwich Village and our now ruined East Dulwich Grove. This is an A road with two bus routes now destined to take up an influx of white vans, lorries, and fast-food deliveries, with pollution rates soaring over WHO guidelines.

My husband had canvassed for the councillor and was stunned when she said to us: "Isn't it wonderful!" He retorted this was the worst thing ever done to us in Dulwich: it was totally unfair and, by virtue of benefiting one set of residents over another, was not in line with Labour policy of equality. "When in a hole stop digging," he advised. "When did the Labour Party become the Green Party?" he pondered.

How did this LTN come about?

In May 2020 then Transport Secretary Grant Shapps had unleashed an LTN bonanza with a £250 million active travel fund for local authorities, but without any overall view about the broader implications for travel patterns across the region.

LTNs were sanitised by a respectable push for safer school routes for children and the benefits of exercise. But it opened the door to sharp lobbyists and disputed research while creating two classes of citizens. "Listen to the people," we urged councillors. All the boundary roads are lined with houses, shops, and, above all, schools. Dulwich is an educational suburb.

East Dulwich Grove, almost a mile long, is THE school road, pavements crammed with children morning and afternoon, educating around five thousand at two elite institutions with preparatory schools and the newish East Dulwich Charter School with playing fields on this boundary. All boundary roads are heavily used by school children.

Yet the council based five miles away seemed not to have considered this. Or the impact on pensioners arriving by bus at the Tessa Jowell Health Centre on

East Dulwich Grove, the 364 residential buildings housing every social stratum, and a nursery for 100 toddlers at the most polluted end.

Climate change by division?

LTN policy is a lesson in how not to do climate change policy, by dividing communities with blatantly obvious discrimination, resulting "In millionaires sitting like Roman Emperors being served by a Labour council," a resident tartly told Catherine Rose, the cabinet minister at Southwark for Parks, Streets, and Clean Air.

Those informed on local council regulation believe they are 'overstepping the mark' into ultra vires territory, dictating social policy by imposing lifestyle changes while raising millions in extra revenue from fines and hiked parking dues, for diversion into what: subsidising a Southwark levelling up policy?

These are national issues which should be overseen by Parliament, not one-party dominated councils instructed by ignorant councillors. Many people believe the draconian restrictions forced on Dulwich were deliberately poorly signposted to generate millions of pounds of income. 'They thought they could get away with it' is a common view.

'Consultation'?

Because of Covid restrictions, opposition from 2020 to early 2022 was muffled by Zoom controlled Council meetings. There was no movement on opening blocked roads to emergency services and disabled people, no consideration of the extra mileage caused by planters, and no additional public transport for an area without a tube. Shops were closing. Care workers fined as they criss-crossed the area. At a scrutiny committee a Transport for London executive intervened when a councillor asked when road charging started: she was incensed many Dulwich residents had two cars on their private driveways. He said carrots are better than sticks.

At another Zoom meeting where harassed mothers complained about problems collecting children due to fines a councillor fantasised about erecting a fountain, another about opening a Sunday vintage market. Dulwich village got a 'parklet' with plants and bench placed over the curb on the road. It was destroyed in a nighttime collision.

'Resistance'?

From early 2021 residents from organised, and from April onwards widely distributed, a series of *Tell Southwark Council* leaflets paid for by individuals, highlighting these issues via the new Dulwich Alliance. Then came posters to stick in windows and gardens. *Clean Air For East Dulwich Grove Too* was my favourite. By May an East Dulwich Grove neighbour invented robust Big Green Posters, using estate agency placards on poles. One-hundred *Stop Road Closures* signs inspired other boundary roads and neighbouring boroughs to copy. Pro-LTNers pulled some down by trespassing into private gardens. A French TV crew visited to film the posters.

Now radicalised, industrious residents began a relentless flow of Freedom Of Information requests.

They bore results. Between the LTN introduction and July 2023, the council has raised £12,990,984 in fines from the Dulwich scheme. We got plenty of media attention.

As required by law Southwark had launched a consultation, ending in July 2021. East Dulwich Grove residents paid for an independent survey: 84 per cent of residents wanted the schemes removed and completely rethought. Two thirds of Dulwich residents wanted the same. The interim result announced in September 2021 tried to hide the scale of opposition. Deliberations continued to the result on 4 January 2022. On 17 February 2022, after protests about how the Dulwich Streetspace measures had adversely affected shops and businesses, the hours of timed restrictions were halved to 2.5 hours. A pathway for emergency services reluctantly opened up, with some concessions for blue badge holders.

'Consultation 2'?

But boundary roads were ignored and have seen no alleviating action. No LTNs were removed. The most hotly contested closed junction, now a fantasy 'Dulwich Square', remained closed to all but emergencies. Before the consultation had ended Southwark council wrote that this was never intended to be a ballot and it would continue to create a network of safe active travel routes.

By 2022 it was clear the resulting traffic schemes had resulted in constant water leaks requiring closures, temporary traffic lights creating jams, accidents, and rerouted buses. The roads open to traffic are completely overloaded. They have no resilience.

Despite the Dulwich campaigns the May 2022 local elections had seen Labour councillors tighten their grip on Southwark while our local Labour MP Helen Hayes failed to take up our case.

LTNs were the dog that did not bark, or so it seemed.

Was the research biased?

This changed in late 2022 and exploded in June 2023, as allegations of biased research were buttressed with video of an academic involved tearing down an anti-LTN poster in a Dulwich shop. The idea that LTNs are the fairest, most efficient way to get people out of their cars is pure fantasy, thundered *The Times*.

The powerful House of Commons Public Accounts Committee joined the fray with a withering report that many LTNs are poorly designed, with next to no idea whether they offer value; many LTNs affect homes for the less well off. Government cash for LTNs was abruptly ended. The opposition to extending Ultra Low Emissions Zones (Ulez) then demonstrated how transport policy and fining could affect elections. Prime Minister Sunak intervened. On 7 June 2023 the Public Accounts Committee unleashed its forthright criticism of LTNs. In July 2023 Transport Secretary Mark Harper stopped funding for new LTNs and ordered a new independent survey. On 30 July 2023 Sunak ordered a review of LTNs and gave a reassuring pro-motorist message to the *Daily Telegraph*.

The Metropolitan Police reported tripled penalty fine appeals for its unmarked cars, wasting 12,266 hours of their time since 2020. There are rush hour queues all over London, including Brixton and Dulwich. Central London has many unexpectedly blocked roads.

Some councils did listen and removed them. After fierce opposition Southwark retreated from an advanced plan to close another residential road in Dulwich Village. It has responded with a scheme for controlled parking zones across the entire borough, aiming to charge residents in wide uncluttered streets and roads £300 a year to park a car outside on the road. This is spreading fury beyond Dulwich.

One view is electric cars will rescue us. That is too long to wait. Climate change is real. Yet so is social injustice, and it does not evaporate either.

Grinding down people into compliance with heavy fines and charges is wrong.

I was once proud of Southwark's recycling policies. I now regard living there as a misfortune.

About the contributor

Maggie Brown was the media editor of *The Independent*, a *Guardian Media* writer, and *Observer* contributor. She is now the Channel 4 historian.

Chapter 16

LTNs: one man, another view, less misery

Christian Wolmar takes a somewhat different view to Maggie Brown's

I am very sorry that Maggie Brown has suffered inconvenience and extra traffic apparently because of the creation of LTNs on neighbouring roads. But she lives on an A road, and A roads are designed to take traffic and her piece hardly amounts to a coherent argument against the concept of LTNs. Her article totally lacks any perspective, or indeed any understanding of how the urban realm needs to be changed in order to repair some of the damage caused by the motorisation of society.

A history lesson

So let me provide it. I'll start with a bit of transport history. The first Ministry of Transport was created in the aftermath of the First World War and it quickly became captured by the growing motoring lobby led by the aristocracy in their deerstalker hats and capes. They wanted the freedom of the roads, and pushed through legislation that provided them with it. The transport budget was largely dedicated to new roads fit for motor vehicles and inevitably that attracted ever more cars. Within a decade the rapid motorisation of society, together with the lack of speed restrictions and other safety considerations, led to a staggering 7,000 deaths in 1930, mostly pedestrians who had the temerity to try to cross the road. This carnage happened, note, at a time when there were just 1.5 million vehicles on the road, fewer than a twentieth of today's numbers.

It took a long time for things to get better.

The Second World War with its petrol rationing and travel restrictions temporarily reduced the numbers travelling on the highways but in the postwar period the car was given precedence over all other forms of transport. Mass car ownership became affordable and the whole panoply of government powers along with almost unlimited amounts of cash created a car-dominated culture that expanded unabated until it came up against its own contradictions.

We got by-passes, dual carriageways, motorways and, disastrously, urban motorways which, in my opinion, wrecked many towns and cities. There was always a clamour for more from the now motorised middle classes backed by politicians who thought the potential of the car to sort out all transport problems was infinite. Meanwhile, bus routes were cut, tramlines scrapped, train lines closed, and even parts of the London Underground were at risk of Beeching-style cuts. The urban environment was redesigned to accommodate cars and people had to squeeze into the small spaces left for them.

Social change or social damage?

The change – damage even - to society was fundamental. Where primary school kids had once universally walked to school, now this was perceived to put their lives at risk; it became impossible to live in rural areas as local buses were scrapped; town centres began to die as out of town supermarkets, only accessible by car, were built . . . and so on.

The fundamental contradiction of motorisation is that it made everyone more mobile but ultimately constrained their ability to move about because of congestion. It is the classic tragedy of the commons, and that is why things had to change. The perceived solution was to build more roads and to give priority to vehicles but the more that these policies were pushed, the more disastrous was the result. Just consider those pictures of fourteen lane highways cutting through cities in the US.

History - all one way?

The tide did, indeed, begin to turn, imperceptibly at first, thanks to a growing recognition that urban spaces were unable to cope with infinite amounts of cars. Something had to give. The towns which had tried to accommodate them by building more and more roads soon found that this was counterproductive. The new roads simply attracted more traffic and filled up and, worse, many pleasant residential roads were turned into rat runs. Radical proposals to create urban motorways began to be politically unacceptable.

In London, for example, there was a proposal for a series of ring roads called motorway boxes, one of which would have gone very near Maggie's house. This would have involved the demolition of some 30,000 homes and turned London into a mini-Los Angeles but fortunately, after a section of it was built in Shepherds Bush, the scheme was abandoned in 1973 due to public opposition. This was in fact a major turning point and one which saved London. The fightback was on and is still continuing.

'A war on motorists'?

Therefore, the more sensible local authorities began to implement a series of measures which have been portrayed as a 'war on motorists' but which in fact began to make their areas more liveable. Parking was restricted and policed by traffic wardens, speed limits were enforced by cameras, buses were given priority with their own lanes, shopping streets were pedestrianised and so on.

There are countless examples of measures which raised controversy at the time but which proved not only popular but boosted local economies.

For example, the A4 used to run right through the middle of Bristol in an area that is now a pleasant square. The Bull Ring in Birmingham, once a series of roundabouts and sections of dual carriageway, was demolished and pedestrianised. Every time an area is pedestrianised or protected from rat-running, the whole atmosphere changed. Opponents were won over. Protesters who were worried local shops would suffer discovered the opposite was true.

People cycling and walking are more likely to spend money locally than motorists who can't be bothered to get out of their cars. Suddenly people discover their neighbours, they find that walking and cycling are once again feasible and local shops and businesses can flourish.

Why the LTNs?

The LTNs which Maggie complains about are part of this wider jigsaw which, when pieced together, is about taming the car. It is not anti-motorist but pro-people. Of course, sometimes schemes are misconceived or don't work out as planned. Some main roads may get an increase in traffic but the name is on the tin – 'main'. That's what they are designed for.

Moreover, there is a well-recognised phenomenon of 'evaporation' as people find other ways to travel. It may not have yet reached Dulwich but again the research confirms that over a longer term it is a widespread phenomenon. intuitively it is obvious since the converse is universally true: new roads or extra lanes on highways fill up with cars almost as soon as they are built.

Therefore LTNs, by reducing through running in some streets – they never block off housing totally unlike what some antis claim – nudge some people into looking at alternatives. Residential roads need to be protected from through running which is not their purpose. Just look at the pictures of these streets from the days before the dominance of motorisation and there are kids playing, neighbours chatting and a sense of tranquillity.

Some motorists are inconvenienced, but it is a small price to pay for what are far wider societal benefits.

This huge change in the nature of the urban realm is an ongoing process of trial and, occasionally error. But overall, this is a process of reclaiming space for people from cars. The benefits come in the form of reduced pollution, health improvements from people exercising more, neighbourliness, reduction of noise and much more.

The other side of the battle

Opponents of these schemes have nothing to offer but more of the same. But a century of favouring the car has delivered urban spaces which, for many, are not only unattractive but almost unliveable. I happen to live in an area (Holloway) where rat running was prevented with a simple semi permeable barrier in the 1980s. When I asked a prominent anti-LTN activist, who has written pieces for the *Daily Telegraph* despite previously being an environmentalist, whether it should be reopened, he said 'yes'. In other words, he thought it preferable for me to live in a street with hundreds or even thousands of cars passing my front door, rather than enjoying the tranquillity of the space created by a previous generation of urban planners. I can happily say that any attempt to reopen the street would be met by protests far larger than anything than the sparsely attended marches mustered by the anti-LTN brigade.

My advice to the anti-LTN warriors

So, Maggie, try to make the best of your local LTN and perhaps there might be a few helpful changes. But please, please, get on the side of those battling to turn our towns and cities into more pleasant places to live. LTNs, Ulez, and 20 mph limits are all about creating urban spaces that accommodate people and prioritise them over heavy pieces of metal hurtling through the streets.

Get on side Maggie, join the campaign to create safer, healthier, and pleasanter neighbourhoods. Work with rather than against your local councillors who genuinely are seeking to improve the lives of their constituents. Some of those horrid cars will then disappear as people shift to walking, cycling, and public transport, and we will be better off and happier. And you may find that actually, living in a car-constrained area, is ultimately a benefit.

About the contributor

One of the UK's leading transport commentators in print and on screen, Christian Wolmar presents *Calling All Stations*, the transport podcast, and is the author of 20 books including *Are Trams Socialist, why Britain has no transport policy* (London Partnership Publishing). Christian is a writer and broadcaster, specialising in transport.

Chapter 17

The Ulez front in the climate culture war

Is opposition to the extension of London's Ultra Low Emissions Zone a symptom of the culture wars or a sign that environmental policy and communications suffer from a democratic deficit? **Philip Hammond** explores

Many commentators were dismayed that the extension of London's Ultra Low Emissions Zone (Ulez) became a culture wars issue in the July 2023 Uxbridge by-election (Harvey 2023). Academics joined in, warning that 'net-zero policies are the next target of right-wing populism and culture wars' (Atkins 2023). A perceived cultural division on climate policy is not confined to the local issue of London's Ulez - *New York Times* columnist Paul Krugman (2023) similarly argues that 'climate is now a culture war issue', for example - and nor is it entirely new (Hoffman 2012). Yet the specifics of today's Ulez debate can clarify the broader dynamics of climate politics and communication.

Culture war?

Casting issues in terms of culture wars often produces more heat than light: the clash of values is rarely well-defined; each side blames the other for starting it; each accuses the other of conspiratorial thinking. Politics has increasingly taken this form over the last decade or so largely because of elite incomprehension at populist revolts against technocratic, expertise-led governance. From that perspective, opposition to Ulez seems ridiculous. As one observer sardonically remarked, 'Fringe right-wing conspiracy theorists [...] view walking around your neighbourhood breathing in fresh air as the latest terrifying assault on our freedoms' (Shadijanova 2023). The benefits of official policy are seen as so self-evident that opposition must be motivated by extremist ideology, disinformation or conspiracy theories.

Viewed from the other side, policies such as Ulez appear as top-down impositions that restrict individual liberty and avoid democratic accountability. In pursuit, supposedly, of a greater good, scare-mongering publicity campaigns are used to induce fear and delegitimise dissent. Since policies are seen to be cooked-up and enforced without open democratic contestation, they are often understood as the outcome of malevolent elite scheming. According to *The Daily Sceptic*, for instance, Ulez is 'just a very small part of a much larger programme to control how our rulers believe we should live our lives' (Craig 2023). As evidence, the article points to London Mayor Sadiq Khan's leading role in C40 Cities, a 'global network of mayors of the world's leading cities that are united in action to confront the climate crisis' (www.c40.org).

Conspiracy hunting

Proponents of the Ulez expansion have tended to smear and discredit their opponents. Mayor Khan claimed that protestors included 'anti-vaxxers [...] Covid deniers, conspiracy theorists, and Nazis', for example (Simpson 2023a). The claim was echoed by the BBC, which characterised protestors as 'far-right conspiracy theorists', though it later backed down after complaints

(Simpson 2023b). A BBC whistle-blower claimed the broadcaster was also colluding with Khan to limit criticism of Ulez, imposing a mandatory editorial referral on all Ulez stories. The senior news producer who leaked the details alleged that the BBC was 'saying one thing publicly [...] while asking staff to act in another way and control the narrative' (Maddox 2023).

Even more damagingly, it emerged that official narrative control was misrepresenting the scientific basis for the policy. A study by researchers at Imperial College (Ma et al. 2021) suggested that in combination with other policies the existing Ulez had contributed to better air quality, but had itself afforded 'only small improvements', the greatest of which was a 'reduction of less than 3% for NO_2 [nitrogen dioxide] concentrations'. Deputy mayor Shirley Rodrigues wrote to a different research group at Imperial (which had received nearly £1m in funding from the mayor's office), saying she was 'really disappointed' with the findings and asking for help to counter them (Rufo 2023).

This repeated a pattern from 2018, when Rodrigues wrote to researchers at Queen Mary University of London asking them to 'reword' their study's finding that there was 'no evidence' of health benefits to children from London's Low Emissions Zone (Knapton 2023). After the Ulez expansion went ahead, a fact-check by *Channel 4 News* calculated that, on the Mayor's own data, it would 'add just 13 minutes to the life expectancy of the average Londoner in 2023' (Lee 2023).

As this indicates, suspicions about elite machinations may not be as far-fetched as the 'conspiracy theorists' label is intended to imply. Take *The Daily Sceptic*'s claims about the ambitions of C40 Cities, for instance. The organisation's own website notes that in his capacity as C40's Chair Khan is 'committed to align C40's budget and staffing behind efforts to tackle air pollution worldwide' and quotes him as hoping to 'fashion a new world after the pandemic'. A 2019 report from C40 Cities, *The Future of Urban Consumption in a 1.5°C World*, outlines several targets for 'consumption interventions' to reduce carbon emissions by 2030. These include 'dietary change', with a 'progressive target' of 16kg of meat and 90kg of dairy consumption per person per year, and an 'ambitious target' of zero meat and dairy consumption; eight new clothing items per person annually (three for the 'ambitious target'); and a reduction in private vehicle ownership to 190 per 1,000 people by 2030, with the ambitious target of zero private vehicles. In this context, it does not seem unreasonable to characterise Ulez as 'part of a much larger programme to control how our rulers believe we should live our lives'. Indeed, others reached similar conclusions about C40's agenda (Kessler 2023, La Terriere 2023).

Serving the public?

Attending Climate Week in New York the month after the Ulez extension, Kahn took to X (formerly Twitter) to argue that 'The most disadvantaged Londoners are suffering the worst consequences of air pollution and the climate crisis'. He wanted, he said, to emphasise 'how important it is to put people at the heart of tackling these twin crises'. Yet acting on behalf of the vulnerable is not the same as acting democratically, and when people were explicitly asked about the expansion of Ulez, they opposed it. In the consultation conducted by Transport for London in 2022, 59 per cent of the public opposed the policy (rising to 68 per cent when responses from campaigners were excluded).

Anti-Ulez groups such as Stop-ULEZ and Truth About ULEZ highlight various problems, including its cost (often understood as a tax-grab by the mayor), and the traffic camera surveillance regime. The core issue, though, is the lack of democratic mandate - which is why the Uxbridge by-election, widely interpreted as a revolt against Ulez, seemed so worrying. Perhaps the clearest example in this respect is the Together Declaration, which originated in opposition to Covid-19 vaccine passports (https://togetherdeclaration.org/about/). It has since taken up other issues, including Ulez, through which a 'draconian, controlling relationship [has] formed with our elected representatives', entailing an 'uninvited restructuring of the social contract'.

A democratic deficit, rather than a culture clash, is at the heart of the conflict over Ulez and other climate policies. Britain's Net Zero policy, adopted in 2019, was not part of any political programme or manifesto offered to the public, for example. Rather, it emerged from an unaccountable quango, the Committee on Climate Change, and passed into law in a matter of weeks. Whatever one thinks of the policy, Britain's Net Zero law clearly bypassed the sorts of democratic decision-making processes that would normally be expected to precede a government passing legislation with such far-reaching implications.

Communications control

In line with such top-down policy-making, officialdom's approach to climate communications has long preferred nudge messaging to open debate and rational argument. The aim, as a Cabinet Office paper explained in 2010, is 'changing behaviour without changing minds' (Dolan et al. 2010). The same year, this strategy became institutionalised in UK governance with the establishment of the Behavioural Insights Team, which continues to advise government, including on 'How to Build a Net Zero Society' using 'incentives' and 'nudges' (Park et al. 2023).

A similar ethos informs broadcasting. All UK broadcasters are members of the environmental organisation Albert, for example, whose 'Planet Placement' initiative counsels programme-makers how to 'shift mindsets and make positive environmental behaviours mainstream' by 'creating content that normalises sustainable behaviours'. Sky even commissioned its own report from the Behavioural Insights Team on 'nudging viewers to decarbonise their lifestyles' via programming that 'makes viewers [...] less likely to argue with information they initially disagree with' (Londakova et al. 2021). Meanwhile *BBC Verify*, like other projects such as the *Trusted News Initiative* or *BBC Reality Check*, hunts down 'climate change denial' on social media networks (Silva and Ahmed 2023).

The problem, for those who wish to control the narrative, is that social media and alternative websites provide a forum for open debate and diverse views - at least for now. Lurid colours on weather maps, scary names for summer heatwaves, or the official announcement of the era of 'global boiling' are routinely questioned and mocked on social networks. Dissident scientists such as Professor Judith Curry - formerly chair of the School of Earth and Atmospheric Sciences at Georgia Tech and a fellow of the American Meteorological Society, who was effectively hounded out of academia under pressure from activists (Rose 2015) - find a wide audience on social media. In this context, characterising disagreement over environmental policies such as Ulez as a culture war waged by extremists is not a description so much as an attempt to quash dissent.

References

Ed Atkins (2023) 'Britain's next election could be a climate change culture war', *The Conversation*, 26 July. Available online at https://theconversation.com/britains-next-election-could-be-a-climate-change-culture-war-210351 (Accessed 29 September 2023)

David Craig (2023) 'The Green Globalists Behind Ulez – and What They Have Planned Next', *The Daily Sceptic*, 31 August. Available online at https://dailysceptic.org/2023/08/31/the-green-globalists-behind-ulez-and-what-they-have-planned-next/ (Accessed 29 September 2023)

Paul Dolan, Michael Hallsworth, David Halpern, Dominic King, and Ivo Vlaev (2010) *MINDSPACE: Influencing Behaviour Through Public Policy*, London: Cabinet Office/ Institute for Government.

Fiona Harvey (2023) 'As Labour loses Uxbridge over Ulez, what now for the party's green policies?' *The Guardian*, 22 July.

Andrew Hoffman (2012) 'Climate Science as Culture War', *Stanford Social Innovation Review*, Vol. 10, No. 4 pp30—37.

Andy Kessler (2023) 'The Climate-Change 'Emergency' Is Coming for You', *Wall Street Journal*, 3 September.

Sarah Knapton (2023) 'Khan's deputy urged scientists to alter study showing emissions scheme had no impact on child health', *The Telegraph*, 22 August.

Paul Krugman, Paul (2023) 'Climate Is Now a Culture War Issue', *The New York Times*, 7 August.

Panda La Terriere (2023)' Mayors' initiative calls for car, dairy and meat ban by 2030', *UnHerd*, 11 September. Available online at https://unherd.com/thepost/mayors-initiative-calls-for-car-dairy-and-meat-ban-by-2030/ (Accessed 29 September 2023)

Georgina Lee (2023) 'Will ULEZ expansion to outer London improve air quality?', *Channel 4 News*, 7 September.

Kristina Londakova, Jake Reynolds, Alice Farrell, Jordan Whitwell-Mak, Elena Meyer zu Brickwedde, Abigail Mottershaw, Tania Loke, and Toby Park (2021) *The Power of TV: Nudging Viewers to Decarbonise their Lifestyles*, London: Behavioural Insights Team.

Ma Liang, Daniel J Graham, and Marc E J Stettler (2021) 'Has the ultra low emission zone in London improved air quality?' *Environmental Research Letters*, Vol. 16, 124001.

David Maddox (2023) 'Whistleblower accuses BBC bosses of 'collusion' with Sadiq Khan to silence ULEZ criticism', *The Express*, 24 June.

Toby Park, Kristina Londakova, Izzy Brennan, Andrew Schein, Jake Reynolds, Ed Whincup, Edwin Chan, Marcos Pelenur, and David Halpern (2023) *How to Build a Net Zero Society*, London: Behavioural Insights Team.

David Rose (2015) '"I was tossed out of the tribe": climate scientist Judith Curry interviewed', *The Spectator*, 28 November.

Yasmin Rufo (2023) 'Ulez: London Mayor accused of "quashing research" questioning the scheme', BBC, 21 August.

Diyora Shadijanova (2023) 'How Conspiracy Theorists Made Air Pollution the Latest Front in the Culture War', *Novara Media*, 15 March.

Marco Silva and Maryam Ahmed (2023) 'The climate change-denying TikTok post that won't go away', BBC, 30 June.

Jack Simpson, (2023a) 'Anti-Ulez protests hijacked by Nazis, says Sadiq Khan', *The Telegraph*, 29 March.

Jack Simpson (2023b) 'BBC admits wrongly claiming far-Right groups attended anti-Ulez protest', *The Telegrap*h, 4 August.

About the contributor

Philip Hammond is Emeritus Professor of Media and Communications at London South Bank University. His books include *Journalism Studies: A Critical Introduction* (with Andrew Calcutt, 2011) and *Climate Change and Post-Political Communication* (2018). He also contributed the chapter on Post-Political Communication and Sustainability to *The Sustainability Communication Reader* (2021).

Chapter 18

The lies they tell

Jon Fuller immerses himself in the UK national press for a week to sample their climate reporting. He comes away unimpressed

I've been active in the environmental movement for 45 years and began to take an interest in the BBC's coverage of issues relating to climate breakdown in the early 1990s. In 2017 I developed the work, forming a group BBC Tell The Truth, working with friends to identify failings within the Corporation and submitting complaints. This aimed to encourage the BBC to do more to educate the public about the gravity of the threats.

When Extinction Rebellion (XR) was formed in May 2018, there was a natural fit between my research and the XR's first demand – Tell The Truth. I spoke at a number of XR's Tell The Truth protest actions, and was part of the XR delegation to meet BBC executives, ITN executives, and other national media editors and staff.

What is the 'truth' in the context of climate change?

The expression 'Tell The Truth' means different things to different people but, to me, there are five core truths:

1. Mass loss of life has begun, but the bulk of the media is reluctant to convey to audiences the full horror of what was happening.

2. The policies that drive climate breakdown are deliberate choices, and those choices cause mass death and suffering; that is criminal in a very literal sense.
3. The risk of runaway climate change is real; there is a grave threat that a series of climate feedbacks could overwhelm our ability to slow global heating, resulting in the sixth mass extinction of wildlife and a collapse in the human population.
4. The 2050 target is far too late. The UK used up its fair share of any carbon budget years ago (the UK has 0.85 per cent of global population but is responsible for 4.52 per cent of global historical emissions).
5. Even if the various climate feedbacks don't overwhelm us, projections for global heating of around 3C by 2100 will result in an unprecedented scale of suffering, mass death, mass displacement and a scale of political upheaval never seen before.

Since 2017, the work of various climate campaigners had nearly driven outright climate denialism out of the mainstream media. In 2023 it is incredibly rare to read pure denialism in the *Daily Mail, Daily Telegraph, Sun*, or *Daily Express,* but they all continue to downplay the suffering caused and gravity of the threat from climate breakdown.

A snapshot: a week of lies

Tasked with analysing one week's output of the UK national papers to show the extent to which readers were being misled, I chose 25 September to 1 October and, sure enough, the findings were typical of every other week.

This was the week after Rishi Sunak's decision to delay a series of interim targets intended to help the UK reach net zero by 2050. It was the week when permission to proceed with the giant Rosebank oil field was announced, when Sunak indicated he would end support for road safety and traffic reduction measures that he perceived as anti-motorist, and when the *State of Nature* report was published by Joint Nature Conservation Committee (JNCC) on the continuing collapse in UK wildlife.

The most obvious example of media deception was a report published by the think tank Civitas, that warned net zero would cost UK households £6,070 per annum up to the year 2050. This was reported on 28 September by the *Sun, Express* and *Mail,* and even by the usually more cautious *Times.* Editors should have known this didn't pass the sanity test, because a mass home insulation programme would greatly reduce energy demand and, if the Conservatives removed all obstacles to cheap onshore wind power in England, the cost of electricity would be greatly reduced.

However, this deception fitted nicely with the anti-net-zero articles being published daily by the mainstream press and it went unchallenged.

On 29 September *The Guardian* published an article that showed why the Civitas report was critically flawed. The paper said: 'Unfortunately the report's author has confused power capacity in megawatts

(MW) with electricity generation in megawatt hours (MWh). As a result, he presents a distinctly unrealistic "£1.3m per MWh" figure for the cost for onshore wind power. The true number is around £50-70/MWh – more than 10,000 times lower. He then compounded his embarrassment by mixing up billions with trillions.'

Civitas then removed the article from its website but, despite that, *The Sun, Express, Mail* and *Times* failed to publish corrections. Worse still, on Sunday 1 October, *The Sun on Sunday* columnist Tony Parsons repeated the figure in an article that praised Rishi Sunak for delaying a number of interim targets intended to help the nation achieve net zero by 2050.

Ulez no thanks

The Telegraph and *Sunday Telegraph* have long campaigned against the net-zero target. Indeed, in one recent edition, *The Sunday Telegraph* published 13 articles opposing net zero and other environmental measures, such as the Ulez expansion in London. The *Sunday Telegraph* recently went so far as to say that Net-Zero was 'un-Conservative'. This theme plays out most days of the *Telegraph* week, with Daniel Hannan, the former MEP, in the *Sunday Telegraph* of 1 October referring to Sunak's decision to delay interim net zero targets as 'The PM is acting precisely as a Conservative should, tackling climate change in a proportionate a cost effective way'.

Right-wing papers have long hurled abuse at climate protesters, with the term 'eco-extremist' and 'eco-clowns' used in connection with a Just Stop Oil protest in the week. The *Daily Star* has a unique twist on this, referring to all climate protesters as 'Tarquin', in an attempt to portray climate activists as upper-class toffs. But the papers don't leave the abuse there. In an attempt to undermine efforts to decarbonising, they even abuse people who support the 2050 target as 'eco-zealots' or 'eco fanatics', with *The Sun's* Trevor Kavanagh (25 September) calling the attempt to reach net-zero as a 'green cult'.

Of course, all this is intended to undermine efforts to decarbonise, thereby allowing the lifestyles of the wealthy to continue unhindered by concerns for the young and those on the frontline of climate breakdown. But that's not enough to stop global efforts to decarbonise at speed. These newspapers have to suppress the most alarming information; and that's where the greatest harm is inflicted upon the nation's understanding of the climate crisis.

Crisis? What crisis?

So, let's turn now to some of the catastrophes that were either not reported or were downplayed by the *Sun*, *Express*, *Mail*, *Star*, *Telegraph* and their ilk.

- Over a year ago 33 million people were severely affected by the record-breaking floods in Pakistan, with much of the water still not having drained away six months later. One year on, the suffering is still continuing. None of these papers have returned to report on the appalling ongoing suffering and the desperate fear that much of Pakistan will become survivable over the coming decades. Millions of people will come to realise they must either move or die.

- In the Horn of Africa, the crisis is the opposite: the sixth year of failed rains has plunged 140 million people into hunger and starvation, killing an estimated 100 thousand people. Again, these papers deny readers the appalling facts, the clear-cut link to climate breakdown, and an implication that is dear to the hearts of many on the right of politics, mass migration of the climate refugees. Hundreds of millions of people on the frontline of climate breakdown would conclude they must either move or die.

- Turning to more recent events, these papers did report (a little) on the record-breaking forest fires in Greece, the impact of Storm Daniel on the country and then, more extensively, on the utter catastrophe caused by Storm Daniel when it hit Derna in Libya. What was missing, however, was an explanation for readers of how these record-breaking events link to climate breakdown, with an abject failure to report what policy experts were saying on the connections with climate change and the future implications.

- These titles didn't explain to readers the significance of the exceptionally warm Mediterranean Sea on the storm as it crossed into Libya and how exceptional the rain was as a consequence. Those papers didn't report on the long-term impacts of Storm Daniel on Greece, and the significance of the second devastating storm two weeks later, Storm Elias.

- Finally, the papers have failed to report to readers the global picture of temperatures close to 1.7C of heating in July 2023, record low ice cover in both the Arctic and the Antarctic, and how these influence the most powerful of climate feedbacks that are now accelerating global heating, the albedo effect of ice and water (ice covered ocean reflects around 90 per cent of the sun's energy back into space, but when it melts, the open ocean appears black from space, absorbing around 90 per cent of the sun's energy).

Had these papers allowed readers to understand the gravity of the various threats, millions of people in the UK would know why we face an unprecedented emergency and why immediate and drastic action is needed to decarbonise. In the absence of responsible reporting, it is left to groups such as XR to focus significant effort on the media in the attempt to get them to tell the whole truth. In my view, it is the single most important part of our endeavour to save all life on Earth.

About the contributor

Jon Fuller has been an active eco-campaigner for 45 years, specialising in energy policy, climate change, and the media. Until 2010 his work was undertaken alongside his role as a civil servant in HMRC's Tax Law Rewrite Project. In the 1990s he ran a small campaign, Speedlimit, that successfully convinced the government to commit to halving the UK's child pedestrian fatality rate. He worked on a variety of local and national campaigns against polluting activities (most notably aviation) and in favour of renewable technologies (most notably the construction of wind farms in Essex). Although a person inclined to respect the law and, despite never having been arrested in his life, Jon agreed to join XR and the non-violent movement of civil disobedience, in the attempt to change government policies and stop mass loss of life associated with climate breakdown. Jon was arrested twice with XR, once beside the pink boat close to BBC Broadcasting House, and the second time outside his former employer's office in Whitehall. After being prosecuted for the protest beside the pink boat, Jon deployed a defence of necessity at his trial, but was convicted. He was not charged after the second arrest because he proved to the police he was arrested unlawfully and the case was dropped. Jon currently leads Climate Genocide Act Now, a group that has proven international criminal law can be used in the context of climate breakdown.

SECTION FIVE

Among the sceptics

Introduction

John Mair

There has always been a strong strain of climate change denial, for which now read climate scepticism in the UK, most especially in the Conservative Party. Physics may have said one thing, but politicians and political writers of the Right said another; the latter simply did not believe the former. The denier/sceptic tendency became outliers after 2016 as the various COPs 'proved' the former and took public opinion with them. That tendency found homes in the more populist, right wing papers like the *Daily Telegraph, Daily Express* and the *Daily Mail.*

The clamour of denial became a whisper. However, in recent years it has had a renaissance especially in the previous berths. Climate sceptics are back. But not in this volume. The editors have attempted to persuade eight sceptics to write for us and you, some of them household names. Not one came forward. Excuses varied from being too busy to simply not replying despite reminders. They are writers who would not write and whose fingers would not touch their keyboards.

Instead, in this brief section, we present some of the critics of the sceptics. Some have been labelled 'eco zealots' by the College of Sceptics. First, Peter York, style guru and President of the Media Society, a 'capitalist tool' by nature but a conspiracy theorist by choice. In 'Climate change activists framed as Maoist oppressors of the poor' he identifies 'The New Enemy' for the Tories – Environmentalists: 'The Conservative party, demoralised by the internal splits over the resignation of Boris Johnson, the disaster of Liz Truss's 44 day prime-ministership, and the Labour party's persistent leadership in the polls, saw their salvation - the New Enemy standing in plain sight. The New Enemy was more relevant than the asylum-seeking boat people, The Trans-Rapist Menace or Black Lives Matter combined. It was all those environmentalists, people who wanted to bankrupt poor ordinary folk by imposing huge extra expenses on them'.

Professor Julian Petley is no fan of the Tories or climate change sceptics. In 'From Brexit to Clexit?' he forensically traces the similarities between the Brexit and the Clexit (denying climate change) campaigns: ideology, tactics, and simply wearing opponents down on the way to victory. They found a willing ear in Prime Minister Rishi Sunak. After his party's surprise win in the Uxbridge and South Ruislip (Boris Johnson's old constituency) by-election on 20 July 2023 on an anti-Ulez platform, the Conservatives discovered a wedge issue with Labour that they hoped would wipe out the massive Labour opinion poll lead and keep them in power after the expected 2024 general election. The sceptics won their case in two months flat. Sunak became a (sophisticated) climate sceptic in his 20 September 2023 postponement of green targets: 'That this mobilisation was able to take place so quickly and effectively bears witness to the presence of deep reservoirs of climate scepticism in the

Tory party which were simply waiting to be tapped. The manner in which the resultant anti-net zero campaign was waged also has resonant parallels with that which produced Brexit – hardly surprisingly, since many of the *dramatis personae* in the former are exactly the same as in the latter'.

Finally, in this section, in 'Boris Johnson, the green shopping trolley' Dr Stephen McCabe of Birmingham City University looks at the much-expressed commitment of the disgraced former Prime Minister to the cause of climate change. It was vintage Boris dissembling once again: 'Whatever Johnson's proclamation of his commitment to dealing with climate change at COP26, prior to becoming PM in 2019, his voting record suggested ambivalence on the issue. Parliamentary vote tracking website *TheyWorkForYou* shows that Johnson 'generally voted against initiatives proposed to reduce the impact of climate change between 2004 and 2020'. As *This Week* reported, in 2019 Johnson voted against a motion calling on the government to bring forward 'a green industrial revolution to decarbonise the economy and boost economic growth' (2021). Additionally, Johnson has never supported any financial incentives to produce low carbon emission electricity'.

So the sceptics may, sadly, not be alive and well in these pages but they are firmly in the ascendant in the Conservative Party and in the dying days of the current Conservative government.

Chapter 19

Climate change activists framed as Maoist oppressors of the poor

Peter York argues that sixty years of fossil fuel company gaslighting on the subject of climate change lies behind the chorus of approval in some UK newspapers for Rishi Sunak's U-turn on the earlier Conservative net zero strategy

Recently an old friend told me how he'd realised what job his father - long dead - had actually done. Growing up he'd never had the word for it. What'd stuck in his mind was that it involved taking people to lunch practically every day. Later he worked it out; his suave, charming dad who'd provided the lovely SW1 house and the school fees in the 1980s was a lobbyist - with the oil industry as a key client. It's taken a while for the rest of us to realise that the climate issue could be urgent, let alone to understand the degree to which we were gaslit about it over the years. Still less who was doing the gaslighting and how they did it.

Dark Money to light the gas?

The backlash/oil industry response to the various iterations of the climate change story is a fascinating microcosm of all Anglosphere dark money network operations. The climate change case is simply stated. First, climate change currently threatens the world; second, it is man-made (anthropogenic); and third, it is fated to worsen disastrously over the next few decades unless we all radically change our behaviour, which probably includes stopping the extraction, processing, and use of fossil fuels. Just Stopping Oil!

But where's the proof? The most relevant evidence seems likely to come not from economists nor politicians nor indeed lobbyists/PRs nor think-tank argument-makers, nor journalists who read history, English, or PPE at Oxford, but from a group that's always called climate scientists. As the decisive expert witnesses there are various measures of their views taken this century in the form of surveys of published climate scientists. According to NASA, a series of studies published in a peer-reviewed *Climate Change 2014 Report*, show that 97 per cent of actively published climate scientists agree that climate warming trends over the past century are extremely likely to be due to human activities.

However, only one in five Americans, in polling conducted in The Yale Programme on Climate Change Communication, June 2023, were aware that this climate scientist consensus exists (it's called The Consensus Gap).

So what's confusing the picture?

In the Robinson Report of 1968 conducted for the US oil producers group, the American Petroleum Institute, the science of man-made climate change was unequivocally confirmed. Research conducted earlier for Exxon, the world's largest oil company, had predicted - according to climate scientists - the impending 'catastrophe' very accurately. (But for internal consumption only; they continued with a public mixture of denial, disinformation, and delays for the following 50 years). The 60-year response from the fossil fuel companies and their investors has involved tens of millions of dollars, hundreds of PR/lobbyists, and partisan think-tanks of all kinds, and, in the US and the UK, a raft of sympathetic media organisations and journalists.

Using 'political technology'

To understand the consensus gap, you have to understand what both Russian experts – and Americans too now - call 'political technology', the modern art and science of getting your way politically. Most people don't, why should they, understand what a K-Street Washington lobbyist does (or his Westminster equivalent). How could they tell the difference between an Astroturf campaign that looks rooted in a community or locality, but is actually something dreamt up, financed, and peopled in the capital by lobbyists, and the real grass roots thing. Or how to evaluate an impressive report from a Westminster think-tank, like the Institute of Economic Affairs. And, if you don't know any national newspaper editors or columnists – and most people don't – why should you know how they work?

Bias in the national media. Why?

The Media Reform Coalition report in 2021 contains a powerful analysis of the skew of British national newspapers, namely that something approaching 80 per cent, by print sales, of British national newspapers are owned by three singular organisations. Those organisations in turn are controlled by three non-dom billionaire right-wing Conservative-supporting proprietors (and according to 2018 Pew research the British national press is the least trusted in Europe).

Ideology

These basic structural or organisational factors aside, what else would incentivise a significant part of the US and UK's legacy and other media to support climate change denial/disinformation stories? There's an ideological strand here. First, the climate change activists are seen as deeply left-wing people who want to use to the climate change story, and its massive uptake amongst Millennials in the West, as a battering ram against capitalism. Second, there's the billionaires club milieu factor. The fossil fuel business – and in particular people like the dark money Koch Brothers (only one left now), who own the second-largest US private company, and are central to the funding of the right-wing billionaires' US political fight back described in Jane Mayer's *Dark Money* (2016) – are at the heart of it. People like the Kochs tend to know and sympathise with their media mogul peers. They have interests in common, like lower taxes and fewer regulations.

Operation

At the newspaper operational level there are two hugely important considerations. The fossil fuel businesses – it's the second-largest business sector in the world, global, long-established, and highly connected - are also very important advertisers for MSM businesses which are still mainly funded by advertising. And many high-profile right-wing print and TV commentators are naturally performative. They haven't built their reputations on analysis, and they never use a graph or do the math if they can help it. They prefer, in print and on-screen, emotive approaches from outright denial – 'it simply isn't happening' (what the oil companies said in the 1970s when they knew it was) to sowing confusion about what's really happening, and when.

'Lefties, oddballs, and weirdos'? How to fight them

There's a related strand in this approach: namely framing climate change activists hard-left as extremists and oddballs (for example, Greta Thunberg's dyslexia). They picture them as over-educated and wildly over-privileged people – the Metropolitan Liberal Elite - who don't understand real people and their problems.

On 21 July 2023, when we had the results of three UK by-elections, the Conservative election campaign planners saw a light at the end of an otherwise disastrous tunnel. They lost two, but they held on to Uxbridge and South Ruislip in London. Everything pointed to a backlash there against the Ulez (Ultra Low Emission Zone). The local Tory opposition had argued furiously that Ulez was a case of crazed posho ideologues forcing real people, ordinary people, to scrap their cars early to buy more expensive, eco-friendly ones.

The new enemy

The Conservative party, demoralised by the internal splits over the resignation of Boris Johnson, the disaster of Liz Truss's 44 day prime-ministership, and the Labour party's persistent leadership in the polls, saw their salvation - the New Enemy standing in plain sight. The New Enemy was more relevant than the asylum-seeking boat people, The Trans-Rapist Menace or Black Lives Matter combined. It was all those environmentalists, people who wanted to bankrupt poor ordinary folk by imposing huge extra expenses on them.

By September 2023 They were ready. Rishi Sunak declared war on what the *Daily Mail* called the 'eco-zealots', by saying he was going to relax the net zero framework set up by Boris Johnson in 2021: 'Brits should not be hit with the £15,000 cost of new cars, boilers and eco-taxes'.

Over the second half of September, the useful media supporters swung into action with this theme in all the newspapers you'd expect (day by day the *Daily Express* headlines looked like Tory *Pravda*) with all of them using 'Brexit Mark 2' language.

'Tackling climate change. It's only for the little people PARP PARP!' said the energetic Richard Littlejohn in *The Mail on Sunday* on 19 September. He explained that all climate change activists were rich hypocrites (or virtue signallers) referencing *The Mail* readers' favourites: The King, Emma Thompson, Mayor Sadiq ('Genghis') Khan, and First Minister Mark Drakeford, to name but a few.

On the 21 September Littlejohn returned to say 'net zero is Brexit Mark 2: the political class versus the people'.

On the 22 September, the *MOS*'s Leo McKinsky joined in, saying 'has any bill ever been as reckless as Ed Miliband's 2008 Climate Act?' He rushed to praise Rishi Sunak's 'pragmatic new approach to reaching net zero by 2050' ('met with fury by the green lobby [...] eco-zealots [...] vast phalanx of unelected green bureaucrats, campaigners and experts').

By the 26 September, Brendan O'Neill, the former Revolutionary Communist Party member and political editor of the Spiked website, was ready with more for the *Mail On Sunday*: 'I was a Sunak Sceptic, but in taking on culture warriors, eco-zealot and sex offenders he has proved he DOES have fire in his belly'. Mr O'Neill (whose site, according to the noted 'eco-zealot' George Monbiot, had received around $300,000 from the Koch Brothers in 2018) couldn't resist referencing the 'culture-war crazies of the virtue-signalling Left'. There's more; they're the 'snooty bourgeois left that looks down its nose at those of us who worry about law and order'.

Look who's talking

Some of these commentators backing the Prime Minister's campaign against 'eco-zealots' (and for 'motorists') clearly have inspired judgment. If we take, for instance, responses to the Truss/Kwarteng budget of September 2022 (generally acknowledged as a huge hit to the British economy of anywhere between £30 and £60bn, and a blow to our national reputation for cool-headedness) *The Mail* was out there on 24 September with an excitable front page headline 'At Last! A True Tory Budget.

And then there's the *Sunday Telegraph's* enthusiastic editor Allister Heath chiming in with 'The furious Blob will try to destroy Rishi Sunak for his net zero heresy', in his paper on 20 September 2023. Mr Heath had experienced a unique revelatory moment last year. On Friday 23 September 2022, he wrote that the Truss/Kwarteng mini-budget 'is a moment in history that will radically transform Britain […] at times, listening to Kwasi Kwarteng I had to pinch myself to make sure I wasn't dreaming'. You can't say fairer than that.

References

BBC (2023) 'By-elections 2023' 21 July https://www.bbc.co.uk/news/uk-politics-66264317

Climate Communication (2023) 'Climate Change and The American Mind: Beliefs and Attitudes, Spring 2023, 8 June https://climatecommunication.yale.edu/publications/climate-change-in-the-american-mind-beliefs-attitudes-spring-2023/toc/2/

Jason Groves (2023) 'Rishi Sunak takes on eco-zealots in a bold move that could transform Tory fortunes and save families up to £15,000 as he hits the brakes on the race to Net Zero', *Daily Mail*, 20 September.

Allister Heath (2022) 'Kwasi Kwarteng's Budget is a moment in history that will radically transform Britain', *The Telegraph*, 23 September.

Richard Littlejohn, *Mail Online* (2023) 18 September.https://www.dailymail.co.uk/debate/article-12532907/RICHARD-LITTLEJOHN-Tackling-climate-change.html

Jane Mayer (2016) *Dark Money,* New York: Doubleday.

George Monbiot, (2018) 'How US billionaires are fuelling the hard-right cause in Britain' The Guardian, 7 December.

NASA (2023) https://climate.nasa.gov/scientific-consensus/

About the contributor

Peter York is a 'capitalist tool' by background, as a market researcher and management consultant. In parallel he is a social commentator, journalist, occasional TV presenter, and author of eleven books, ranging from the best-selling *Official Sloane Ranger Handbook* to *Authenticity is a Con*, an attack on the cult of authenticity. His latest book, co-written with Professor Patrick Barwise, is *The War Against the BBC* (Penguin 2020). He is the President of The Media Society.

Chapter 20

From Brexit to Clexit?

Julian Petley detects a considerable overlap between Tory Brexiters and climate sceptics, both in terms of the MPs involved and the ideas which motivate them. Similarly, those newspapers which clamoured for Brexit have been equally determined to demand that the government weakens its climate policies

In the June 2023 Uxbridge by-election, the perceived unpopularity of mayor Sadiq Khan's expansion of London's Ultra Low Emission Zone (Ulez) to the city's outer boroughs was successfully mobilised by the Tories in order to engineer the victory of their candidate, albeit with a majority of only 495 votes, reduced from 7,210 in 2019. Climate-sceptic Tory MPs then immediately pressured the government to roll back its net zero policies. This in spite of the awkward facts that (a) Ulez is not a net zero policy, its purpose being to improve air quality, not to reduce carbon emissions; and (b) it was first announced in July 2014 by Boris Johnson when he was London mayor, and backed by then prime minister David Cameron.

'Two sides of the same ugly coin'?

That this mobilisation was able to take place so quickly and effectively bears witness to the presence of deep reservoirs of climate scepticism in the Tory party which were simply waiting to be tapped. The manner in which the resultant anti-net zero campaign was waged also has resonant parallels with that which produced Brexit – hardly surprisingly, since many of the *dramatis personae* in the former are exactly the same as in the latter. And as Matthew d'Ancona (2023) observed in *The New European*: 'Politically, psychologically and strategically, the two projects are intimately connected. They are two sides of the same ugly coin'.

Many of those who clamoured for Brexit were already climate change deniers. They include: Lord Lawson, founder of the Global Warming Policy Foundation (GWPF); Matt Ridley, coal owner, *Times* columnist and GWPF advisor; Owen Paterson, fired as environment secretary in David Cameron's July 2014 cabinet reshuffle after giving a speech to the GWPF (partly written by brother-in-law Ridley) in which her argued that the 'Climate Change Act should be effectively suspended and eventually repealed'; and James Delingpole, former executive editor of *Breitbart London* who on his website describes his dislikes as including 'the European Socialist Superstate' and 'the "global warming" myth'.

The winter floods of 2015-2016 provided these and others with unrivalled opportunities to bang both the climate change denialism and the Brexit drums. For example, Delingpole, writing in *The Sun*, 31 December 2015, in an article headed 'EU know who did this to Britain', blamed the flooding not on climate change but on the European Water Framework Directive, which discouraged dredging. Thus the real causes of the disaster were 'our unelected masters in Brussels [...] driven by lunatic green ideology'. A similarly line was taken by Ridley's column in *The Times*, 4 January 2016, titled 'Don't blame climate change for these floods', in which he accused the British government of 'gold-plating' the Directive, which, he helpfully pointed out, also marked 'one of the first times the European Union invited the big green environmental organisations to get directly involved in policymaking'.

Clexit

Indeed, after the Brexiters' success in the Referendum, a new group by the name of Clexit was formed. Its 1200 word founding statement declaimed that 'Brexit was Britain's answer to the growing over-reach of EU bureaucracies. Clexit is our answer to the push for global control through climate hysteria' and stated: 'Nations should not tolerate UN and EU bureaucrats manipulating science in order to justify their dreams to redistribute wealth and revert to the central planning that enslaved and impoverished the old command economies' (quoted in Readfearn 2016).

As is the case with so many organisations of this type, Australian and American mining and petro-chemical interests loomed large among the membership, but in the present context it's worth noting that its first president was arch-denialist Christopher Monckton. He had joined UKIP in 2009 and then became its chief spokesperson on climate change followed by its deputy leader, head of its policy unit and its president in

Scotland, although he was sacked by Nigel Farage in November 2013 in a bout of factional infighting.

Elective affinities

More recently, the elective affinities between so-called Euroscepticism and climate scepticism have become abundantly clear in the overlapping memberships of the European Research Group (ERG) and the Net Zero Research Group (NZRG), and are epitomised by figures such as Steve Baker MP and Craig Mackinlay MP.

In 2015 Baker co-founded Conservatives for Britain (president: Lord Lawson), whose purpose was to lobby for an EU referendum, and from 2016-2017 and 2019-2020 he was chairman of the ERG. In May 2021, he joined the Board of Trustees of the GWPF and, ahead of the COP26 climate summit, he and Mackinlay set up the NZRG, which brings together backbench Conservative MPs who oppose many of the government's net zero policies. This has very close links with the Institute of Economic Affairs, a powerful pro-Brexit think tank which has long opposed government climate policy. Baker has also written articles critical of the costs of these policies for Net Zero Watch, a campaign launched and managed by the GWPF.

Mackinlay was one of the founders of the Anti-Federalist Party, the forerunner of UKIP, serving as the latter's leader in 1997 and as deputy leader from 1997-2000 before joining the Conservative Party in

2005. He was a founding member of Conservatives for Britain, and in the 2015-2017 and 2017-2019 parliaments was a member of the Exiting the EU Select Committee. In the 2015-2017 parliament, he was also a member of the European Scrutiny Select Committee. On the climate front, he leads the NZSG and since 2020 has chaired the All-Party Parliamentary Group (APPG) for Fair Fuel for UK Motorists and Hauliers. A prominent member of that group is Howard Cox, the founder of motoring lobby group Fair Fuel UK, which is a vocal opponent of fuel duty increases and the government's 2030 (now 2035) ban on the sale of new petrol and diesel vehicles. He is running as the Reform Party candidate in the 2024 London mayoral election on a pledge to scrap Ulez entirely and to remove Low Traffic Neighbourhoods.

Self-fulfilling prophecies

Given this fusion of concerns amongst a significant number of Tory MPs, and the vociferous support which they have received from the right-wing press, it is entirely unsurprising that climate change has risen so rapidly up the political agenda. Indeed, in January 2022 Baker disingenuously predicted that this is precisely what would happen (and then ensured that it did) when interviewed for Sky News: 'I genuinely believe that when the full costs of net zero start hitting us, if people have never been given a choice at the ballot box, we could end up with something bigger than the poll tax, certainly bigger than Brexit, because the numbers of people hit by it and their inability to cope will be huge' (Quoted in Thomas-Peter 2022).

He made a similar point in *The Sun*, 25 May 2021, when, in a clear echo of the arguments made for the EU referendum, he complained that the 'elite policymakers who govern our lives' had not been upfront about the cost of net zero and that 'you, the voter, have not had a choice'. In his view, if the Tories lost touch with their voters and 'forced the public into buying expensive, ineffective heating' and made us 'give up our cars, we will reap what we have sown. The cost of Net Zero could deliver a political crisis greater than the Poll Tax'.

Culture wars

However, this is a culture war issue as much as it is an economic one, however hard the Tories, and what Tim Bale (2023: 4) fittingly calls the 'party in the press', try to persuade us that they're trying to protect the poor – which, to put it mildly, would be uncharacteristic. So what are the ideological factors in play here? A distrust of expert opinion, dislike of international treaties and top-down government interventions, paranoia about the activities of 'metropolitan liberal elites', and fear that personal freedom is in peril from a form of creeping socialism – or worse, in the form of the Great Reset. And, entirely unsurprisingly, these sentiments have been amplified by exactly the same right-wing newspapers that supported the Covid libertarians.

Discourses of climate delay

Up until around 2016, climate change denial was a staple of papers such as the *Sun*, *Telegraph*, *Mail*,

Express, and their Sunday equivalents. However, as a highly detailed analysis by Carbon Brief (Gabbitas et al. 2021) has demonstrated, outright denialism has given way to scepticism (of a kind) and it should be noted this has very significantly increased since the study concluded in 2021, particularly in the wake of the fuel price rises caused by the Ukraine war. Specifically, there have been attacks on climate activists, complaints that the UK is doing too much and other countries too little, and growing criticisms of the cost, particularly to that Tory staple, 'hard-working families', of achieving net zero by 2050.

These are examples of what have come to be called 'discourses of climate delay' [which] accept the existence of climate change, but justify inaction or inadequate efforts. In contemporary discussions on what actions should be taken, by whom and how fast, proponents of climate delay argue for minimal action or that action should be taken by others. They focus attention on the negative social effects of climate policies and raise doubt that mitigation is possible (Lamb et al. 2020).

The effect, and almost certainly the intention, is, as d'Ancona points out, to 'undermine the public and political consensus on climate change, to sow the seeds of doubt and to create political division'.

This is exactly the line pursued by Net Zero Watch (2023), which states on its website: 'We will scrutinise policies, establish what they really cost, determine who will have to pay, and explore affordable alternatives

[…] We all want to see a cleaner and better environment for future generations, but if climate and energy policies are rushed and their costs and implications not fully thought through, they will almost certainly do more harm than good'.

And this approach is faithfully echoed to the letter by the climate-sceptic newspapers. To take but one example from myriad possible ones, a *Daily Mail* leader, 30 March 2023, proclaims: 'No one denies global warming. But the UK is responsible for just 1 per cent of global CO2 emissions. We need policies based on rational analysis, not the hysteria of climate alarmists. We need to ensure energy security and not impoverish ourselves. Our green dream must be the springboard for a leap forward – not a leap in the dark'.

Harbingers of the future?

This is all straight out of the disruptors' playbook, and it was precisely by such means that Brexit was pushed gradually but remorselessly up the political agenda from the mid-1990s onwards. Now Nigel Farage and Reform Party leader Richard Tice are agitating for a net zero referendum, with papers such as the *Daily Telegraph* (whose climate-sceptic columnist Allison Pearson the paper doesn't inform us is a director of the GWPF) are taking up the call. So, for example, in a column on 22 September 2023 headed 'Nobody ever asked us if we wanted green energy. They just did it', Kathryn Porter, commenting on Sunak's modifying of the Tories net zero policies, suggested that: 'Perhaps the Prime Minister has recognised, as Nigel Farage has been saying for some time, that there has been a democratic deficit around net zero that is similar to the deficit that eventually led to the Brexit vote. Because, as with EU membership, political elites have taken us down the road to net zero without waiting to see if this is a road we, the public, wish to travel'.

Significantly, one of the places in which Farage delivered his thoughts on this subject was in the same paper on 17 January 2023, in which he opined that 'I cannot think of an issue on which the Westminster class, along with their media friends, are more out of touch with the rest of the country. It is time MPs got off their high horses and listened to some common sense'.

Don't say you haven't been warned.

References

Tim Bale (2023) *The Conservative Party after Brexit*, Cambridge: Polity.

Matthew d'Ancona (2023) 'The Eurosceptics are now ecosceptics .. this time they will wreck the planet', *The New European*, 16 August.

Josh Gabbatis, Sylvia Hayes, Joe Goodman, and Tom Prater (2021) *Analysis: How UK Newspapers Changed Their Minds about Climate Change*. Available at https://interactive.carbonbrief.org/how-uk-newspapers-changed-minds-climate-change/

William F. Lamb et al. (2020) 'Discourses of climate delay', 'Discourses of climate delay', *Global Sustainability*, 3, E17. Available at https://www.cambridge.org/core/journals/global-sustainability/article/discourses-of-climate-delay/7B11B722E3E3454BB6212378E32985A7

Net Zero Watch (2023) 'Who we are'. Available at https://www.netzerowatch.com/who-we-are/#:~:text=Net%20Zero%20Watch%20highlights%20the,pay%2C%20and%20explore%20affordable%20alternatives.

Graham Readfearn (2016) 'After Brexit, climate science denialists form new group to call for a clexit', DeSmog, 3 August. Available at: https://www.desmog.com/2016/08/03/after-brexit-climate-science-denialists-form-new-group-call-clexit/

Hannah Thomas-Peter (2022), 'Net zero targets could cause more unrest and division than Brexit, Tory MP warns', 21 January.

About the contributor

Julian Petley is Honorary and Emeritus Professor of Journalism at Brunel University London. He is a member of the editorial boards of the *British Journalism Review* and *Ethical Space*, and a frequent contributor to *Byline Times*, among other independent publications. *The Routledge Companion to Freedom of Expression and Censorship*, which he co-edited with John Steel, will be published in December 2023.

Chapter 21

Boris Johnson, the green shopping trolley

Steven McCabe looks at the track record of former Prime Minister Boris Johnson and asks whether on this, as on many issues, he is a shopping trolley veering from side to side

The eco warrior?

Arguably, the most significant contribution to climate change by Boris Johnson was his address to world leaders as PM at the United Nations COP26 conference in Glasgow on 1 November 2021 (Gov.uk, 2021). Delivered in typically rambling prose, including reference to Scotland's 'most globally famous fictional son' - James Bond! - he stressed the belief that there was only a minute to go on the doomsday clock. Urgent action, Johnson claimed, was essential.

When Johnson stated that 'we've learned not to ignore [scientists]' on climate change, some listening to him may have raised an eyebrow. From what we know of Johnson's character (McCabe, 2021), this is a politician for whom the opinions of all others, including scientists, may be used (and abused) as long as they conveniently comply with his required narrative.

Nonetheless, Johnson was unequivocal that the agreement on climate achieved at COP26 was a 'big step forward' and would 'mark the beginning of the end of climate change' (Reuters, 2021). Subsequent to his speech in Glasgow, Johnson acknowledged the huge amount of work needed to avert an existential crisis for billions of people. Pointedly, he committed himself to working 'tirelessly' to ending climate change (Prime Minister's Office, 13 November 2021).

In making comparison with the somewhat cavalier and detail-free way Johnson handled negotiations with the European Union to achieve a deal to leave, in a *New Yorker* article, Sam Knight contends, 'Our planetary catastrophe is not salvageable, or bluffable, in the same way' (2023). Knight identifies Johnson's previous statements on climate change. Though a change of view is to be applauded, Johnson's conversion to the cause of climate change is Damascene in comparison to his previously stated views on this issue.

Does Johnson really believe in the 'green crap'?

In November 2012 former PM David Cameron who'd promised the 'greenest government ever' (Bennett, 2016) reportedly instructed aides to 'get rid of all the green crap' from energy bills. Boris Johnson had voiced scepticism more publicly. Whilst London mayor, Johnson wrote a regular column for the *Daily Telegraph* where he stated his willingness to entertain arguments both for and against climate change (2013). Johnson admitted he wished he knew more about the subject. Peculiarly, however, the expert he wrote of having consulted for guidance was climate change denier Piers Corbyn (brother of Jeremy). In his conclusion Johnson muses that 'speaking only as a layman', whether the government should consider entertaining 'the possibility – however remote – that Corbyn is right'. Many eminent scientists took issue with what they regarded as Corbyn's unsubstantiated by evidence speculation (Hickman, 2013).

In December 2015, once again in his *Telegraph* column, Johnson considered the unseasonably mild weather the country was experiencing. He asserted that the belief held by many that global warming was causing temperatures to increase was a 'primitive fear'. That fear, he explained, 'as far as I understand the science – is equally without foundation'. As before, Johnson quoted the 'great physicist and meteorologist Piers Corbyn'.

Whatever Johnson's proclamation of his commitment to dealing with climate change at COP26, prior to becoming PM in 2019, his voting record suggested ambivalence on the issue. Parliamentary vote tracking website *TheyWorkForYou* shows that Johnson 'generally voted against initiatives proposed to reduce the impact of climate change between 2004 and 2020'. As *This Week* reported, in 2019 Johnson voted against a motion calling on the government to bring forward 'a green industrial revolution to decarbonise the economy and boost economic growth' (2021). Additionally, Johnson has never supported any financial incentives to produce low carbon emission electricity.

Little wonder that, according to *Forbes*, a number of those involved in organising the UN climate summit in Glasgow were concerned at how genuine was Johnson's conversion to the need for climate change (Keating, 2020). Notably, in January 2020, Johnson's energy minister Claire O'Neill was replaced by him as president of the COP26 conference. When interviewed by the BBC she accused Johnson of merely using climate change for politics rather being focused on ensuring realistic and workable solutions to reduce carbon emissions (BBC, 20200). She added that Johnson admitted to her 'he doesn't really understand it [climate change]', which might suggest doubters of Johnson's sincerity on the issue were right to be suspicious.

Johnson the flip-flop man

Johnson's ability to alter his stance on issues is not surprising (Gimson, 2023). Many have alleged his relationship with facts and the truth is highly negotiable. His former boss at *The Telegraph*, Sir Max Hastings wrote an excoriating piece on the man about to become PM (2019). Johnson's inclination to those with considerable wealth – and willing to donate to his campaigns – is well known. As website *LittleSis* shows, billionaire hedge fund manager Sir Michael Hintze, who provided financial support to climate science denial group the Global Warming Policy Foundation, donated £5,000 in the 'run up to Boris Johnson's 2008 May London Mayoral Election' (2023).

Having been re-elected as MP for Uxbridge and South Ruislip in 2015, and as foreign secretary from 2016, Johnson demonstrated a distinct lack of interest in climate change. Memorably, though vocal in opposing a third runway at Heathrow airport and stating his intention to 'lie down in front of those bulldozers', he conveniently missed the vote with what was regarded as a 'hastily arranged diplomatic trip' to Kabul (Buchan, 2018). Research by *This Week* showed that in his time as foreign secretary, the number of full-time officials devoted to climate change in the Foreign Office declined by 'almost 25% in two years' (*ibid*). As reported by the *Guardian* in April 2018, Johnson had not made any reference to climate change in any official speech since taking up his role as Foreign Secretary (Carrington, 2018).

Open Democracy as part of its 'Dark money' series reported that, prior to becoming PM in 2019, Johnson received £25,000 from a climate change denier to support his successful bid to become leader of the Conservative Party (Geoghegan, 2019). The money was donated by First Corporate Shipping, the trading name of Bristol Port, co-owned by Terence Mordaunt. Geoghegan explains that Mordaunt was then director of the Global Warming Policy Forum, the advocacy arm of the climate sceptic Global Warming Policy Foundation, and accused of 'giving a platform to fringe climate science deniers', through its high-profile Westminster connections (*ibid*).

Brazilian boxer Vitor Belfort's observation that 'legacy is not what you do for yourself but what you achieve for the next generation' is apposite to the challenge faced by politicians in confronting climate change. Significantly, in Johnson's time as PM he can claim to have achieved much in terms of policy on climate. Publication of the 'Ten Point Plan for a Green Industrial Revolution' (HM Government, 2020) represents a coalescence of strategy under Johnson in the quest for net zero. His endorsement of the plan is unequivocal. Greenpeace recognised Johnson's leadership with the UK having 'some of the strongest climate targets in the world' (2022). Notably, following PM Rishi Sunak's announcement to alter the timetable for many green initiative commitments made previously, Johnson has been vocal in condemning this move and urged him not to 'falter' (BBC, 2023).

Can Alex the gadfly be believed?

Attempting to fully understand what Boris Johnson really believes – Alexander is his first name – is not straightforward. As his hero, wartime leader Sir Winston Churchill said of Russia in an October 1939 radio broadcast, he's something of 'a riddle wrapped in a mystery inside an enigma'. Johnson's persona is based on an act he's been perfecting since his time as a teenager being bullied at Eton and regarded as too 'bookish' (Docx, 2021; McCabe, 2022). Though the moniker 'shopping trolley' used to refer to Johnson is credited to former chief of staff Dominic Cummings, once acknowledged as being his Svengali, it came from his own lips about his indecisiveness of which side to back in the 2016 EU referendum.

Those who've studied Johnson closely contend he possesses no fixed ideology. As a political 'gadfly' he employs issues on the basis of whether they're politically expedient and, as a consequence, veers around like a shopping trolley without direction (Rentoul, 2022). Based on his statements over the last 15 years, Johnson's commitment to the cause of climate change may be considered to be a case in point. As PM he claims he was convinced by scientists of the need for urgent action (Climate Brief, 2022). Without evidence to the contrary, we have to believe his conversion to being committed to climate change is sincere. However, given what we know of the man

(Bower, 2021), it's hard not to conclude that were he still PM and experiencing dire opinion polls in the way Sunak is at present, he'd happily dump policies he proclaimed in November 2020 as essential to deal with the 'most enduring threat to our planet'.

References

BBC (2020) 'Criticism after UK climate envoy Claire O'Neill is replaced', BBC Politics Website, 31 January, https://www.bbc.co.uk/news/uk-politics-51331167 (Accessed 20 September)

Craig Bennett (2016) 'David Cameron promised the greenest government ever – and failed. Now Theresa May is following his lead', *Independent*, 14 July.

Tom Bower (2021) *Boris Johnson: The Gambler,* London: WH Allen.

Lizzy Buchan (2018) 'Boris Johnson faces calls to resign after jetting off to Afghanistan to dodge crucial Heathrow vote', *Independent*, 25 June.

Damian Carrington (2018) 'Foreign Office climate staff cut by 25% under Boris Johnson', *Guardian*, 25 April.

Climate Brief (2022) 'Revealed: The 11 slides that finally convinced Boris Johnson about global warming', Climate Brief Website, 1 February, https://www.carbonbrief.org/revealed-the-11-slides-that-finally-convinced-boris-johnson-about-global-warming/#:~:text=Johnson%20admitted%20he%20ha d%20been,it's%20very%20hard%20to%20dispute. (Accessed 22 September.)

Edward Docx (2021) 'The clown king: how Boris Johnson made it by playing the fool', *The Guardian*, 18 March.

Peter Geoghegan (2019) 'Tory hopefuls under fire for accepting cash from company linked to major 'climate science denial' group', Open Democracy, 12 June https://www.opendemocracy.net/en/dark-money-investigations/revealed-climate-change-denier-makes-big-donation-boris-johnson-and-jeremy-hunt/ (Accessed 21 September)

Andrew Gimson (2023) *Boris Johnson: The Rise and Fall of a Troublemaker at Number 10,* London: Simon & Schuster.

Gov.uk (2021) 'PM address at COP26 World Leaders Summit Opening Ceremony', Gov.uk, 1 November, www.gov.uk/government/speeches/pm-address-at-cop26-world-leaders-summit-opening-ceremony (Accessed 19 September)

Greenpeace (2022) 'The verdict on Boris Johnson's green track record – and what he should do next', Greenpeace Website, 15 July, https://www.greenpeace.org.uk/news/boris-johnson-green-record/ (Accessed 22 September)

Max Hastings (2019) 'I was Boris Johnson's boss: he is utterly unfit to be prime minister', *The Guardian*, 24 June.

HM Government (2020) Ten Point Plan for a Green Industrial Revolution', HM Government Website,

November 2020, https://assets.publishing.service.gov.uk/government/uploads/system/uploads/attachment_data/file/936567/10_POINT_PLAN_BOOKLET.pdf (Accessed 22 September)

Leo Hickman (2013) 'Boris Johnson says snow casts doubt on climate change science', *Guardian*, 21 January.

Boris Johnson (2013) 'It's snowing, and it really feels like the start of a mini ice age', *Telegraph,* 20 January.

Boris Johnson (2015) 'I can't stand this December heat, but it has nothing to do with global warming', *Telegraph*, 20 December.

Dave Keating (2020) 'Four Years Ago, Boris Johnson Said Climate Concern Was 'Without Foundation'', Forbes website, 5 February, https://www.forbes.com/sites/davekeating/2020/02/05/four-years-ago-boris-johnson-said-climate-concern-was-without-foundation/?sh=4e647f3e6954 (Accessed 20 September)

Sam Knight (2021) 'Boris Johnson's Fickle Climate Leadership', *The New Yorker*, 4 November.

LittleSis (2023) 'Donation: Michael Hintze, Boris Johnson', LittleSis Website, https://littlesis.org/relationships/1123526 (Accessed 21 September)

Steven McCabe (2021), 'Al promised you a miracle – Life under 'Greased Piglet' Johnson', in *Populism and the Media*, edited by John Mair, Tor Clark, Neil

Fowler, Raymond Snoddy, and Richard Tait, Bury St Edmunds: Abramis Academic Publishing.

Steven McCabe (2022) 'What's in a name? How Alexander de Pfeffel became Boris', in *Boris Johnson: Media Creation, Media Clown, Media Casualty*, edited by John Mair, Andrew Beck, and Paul Connew, Oxford: MGM.

Reuters (2021) 'UK's Johnson says climate deal is a big step forward', Reuters News Website, 14 November, https://www.reuters.com/business/cop/uks-johnson-says-climate-deal-is-big-step-forward-2021-11-13/ (Accessed 19 September)

About the contributor

Dr. Steven McCabe is an Associate Professor at Birmingham City University. He writes and comments regularly in the national and international media on politics and the economy. In the past three years he has edited a number of books including *Brexit and Northern Ireland, Bordering on Confusion, Exploring the Green Economy – Issues, Challenges and Benefits*, *Green Manufacturing, what this involves and how to achieve success*, and *Another Way, an Examination of Britain's Defence Policy*. More recently, he co-edited *India at 75*.

SECTION 6

Storm warning

Introduction

John Ryley

We end by turning towards the future of climate journalism. The very best journalism dares to challenge the accepted narrative, dares to ask awkward questions, and dares to stand up to authority. Journalists will need to stick close to these principles during the next decade as the impacts of climate change get faster, become more intense and more central to political decision-taking. Let's be clear. The golden age of journalism is now and even more so in the immediate future. The constant technological revolution has made this a better time to be a journalist than ever before. It means we have more new tools at our disposal than ever, not just to report events as they happen but to analyse, explain them and put them in context. The pessimists who look backwards to some mythical golden age of old-fashioned journalism are mistaken. We will need these tools to ensure our reporting is questioning, robust, and independent as the climate change story becomes even more centre-stage.

Here are three recommendations to try to make climate journalism better in an age of disinformation.

Improve climate literacy

To get the science right newsrooms need to have a thorough understanding of climate change just as they do of other specialisms such as politics, economics, or sport. Not just the basics, for example knowing the difference between climate mitigation and adaption but also equipped with the wherewithal to interrogate the evidence, question the experts' views, and expose falsehoods. Just as newsrooms in the 1980s and 1990s ran courses to make economic journalism better so too will classes need to be held to explain the science of climate change.

Concrete suggestions on the teaching of climate journalism are put forward by Professor Chris Paterson at the University of Leeds. He says the ‘next generation of journalists will all be environmental journalists, telling daily stories of climate emergency. Ignorance or denial will no longer be an option, even for media outlets which previously chose that path'. To highlight the 'absurdity of false balance' he encourages teachers to ask their students to report another field of science and then requiring them to find someone to deny what they discover.

Make the most of data

Numbers don't lie - they reveal stories. One of the unshakable tenets of the digital revolution is Amara's Law. Coined by Roy Amara, a Stanford computer expert, the rule states 'We tend to overestimate the effect of technology in the short run and underestimate the effect in the long run'. The use of accurate data - its patterns and variations - is transforming the ability of journalists to hold institutions, governments, and politicians to account as we saw in the recent Covid pandemic. Day in day out, trained journalists equipped with the data can chip away at the public relations shields which the establishment erects around itself by asking awkward questions and unpicking the data. And, as the likes of the *Financial Times'* James Burn-Murdoch and Sky's Ed Conway have demonstrated so well, the complex data can be compressed into a graphic or chart with a simple story. Persistent, tenacious inquiry is the rock on which good journalism is based. Climate journalism will be able to offer a depth of analysis not seen before, both to diagnose and suggest solutions, thanks to journalists having better, sharper tools than ever before.

Commit to eye-witness reporting

Putting journalists at the heart of the story who can credibly bear witness to what is really happening is the core of great journalism whatever the story. Video journalism enables journalists to capture the changing nature of our climate up close. But it's not cheap. To reinforce the significance of eye-witness reporting we conclude this book with two reports from the front line of climate change. The first from China, the world's largest carbon emitter, the second from the Maldives in the India Ocean, the world's lowest-lying country.

While the U.K.'s progress on meeting its targets is important, no pledge is as significant as the People's Republic of China. China is the world's largest energy consumer and carbon emitter, accounting for one-third of all global CO2 emissions. It will be China who sets the pace if the world wants to prevent global warming exceeding 1.5c.

From the city of Shanghai, in a series of impressionistic vignettes, Andrew Beck observes that newspapers are a very rare sight. China, he says, is very focused on promulgating the benefits of green energy. He describes how the lead director for the opening ceremony of the 2023 Asian Games in the city of Hangzhou proclaimed, 'Hangzhou is a very special city. It's one of the best places to show the whole world China wants to take the responsibility to help save the earth, to save the planet [...] it's so green'. Beijing has a coherent industrial policy: patrol vehicles are given a limited number of days to enter cities; the drivers of electric vehicles get given their number plates much quicker than those who drive petrol cars; and to reduce reliance on fossil fuels, the Chinese government closed coal mines in the big coal processing province of Shanxi but, unlike the UK, Beijing compensated redundant coal miners and funded the retraining of former coal miners.

Almost 6000 kilometres away Dr Alan Geere has filed a piece from the Maldives' capital Male. He reports that the 26 atolls will be uninhabitable by 2100 if the sea continues to ride at its current levels. He finds that climate issue was not an issue taken seriously by any of the eight candidates in the presidential elections in September 2023 despite the threat from the Indian ocean. He hears from a prominent local journalist who says 'many journalists, particularly at the editor level, don't understand the intricacies of the climate crisis or the geographical vulnerabilities well enough to discern or translate into general reporting how multifaceted the problem is', and suggests the way to focus her fellow local journalists' attention might be to offer bespoke grants and collaborations with international news outlets.

Visual storytelling

We live an age of visual story telling like no other. Pictures - video and stills - can be combined with text, graphs, and audio to tell compelling stories. Video presents a big opportunity for climate journalism - a chance to pioneer. In the years ahead the reporting of climate change will show the real value of careful, data driven journalism provided by accurate, independent, trusted news organisations who invest in visual journalism. Remember: journalism is often a first draft of history.

Chapter 22

Educating for climate change

How do we teach the next generation of journalists to report climate change responsibly? **Chris Paterson** of Leeds University has some concrete suggestions

The next generation of journalists will all be environmental journalists, telling daily stories of climate emergency. Ignorance or denial will no longer be an option, even for media outlets which previously chose that path. Globally, journalism education sits at an intersection of two forces: a clarion call for action to address a climate emergency that is ever more present in the public imagination, and a nascent embrace of environmental reporting by all but the most entrenched climate change denying media outlets. It is a time for what Hackett called 'ordinary journalism in extraordinary times' (Hackett et al 2017: 1).

Journalism educators face the challenge of all educators in determining how to integrate climate change in their teaching, but with the knowledge that their lessons will affect how climate change is communicated to the public in the decades to come.

Wide agreement that everyone, educators included, should be talking about climate change, is unfortunately mirrored by widespread reluctance to do so. As climate journalist David Roberts explained in a Ted Talk a decade ago, 'thought leaders' have tended to avoid the topic. He paraphrases one such unnamed 'prominent pundit' as saying, "It seems really complicated, I don't feel like I have a good grasp on all the science and so I just don't feel qualified to go out and assert things publicly about it." Roberts (2012) adds that 'anytime you mention it (on social media) the hordes descend, bearing complicated stories about the mediaeval ice age, or sunspots, or water vapour [...] there's a lot of myths about climate change borne by these climate sceptics, but to debunk those myths [...] you have to research to respond to them in detail' and people don't bother.

His talk, like Al Gore's presentations a decade earlier, sought to demonstrate that the science is, in fact, straightforward and clear. The task is urgent and, for professional communicators like Roberts, surprisingly difficult, due to manufactured structures of obfuscation, confusion, and denial. It is the mission of educators to, firstly, equip their students with the confidence to understand the parameters of the problem and speak confidently about it and, secondly, understand the nature of the communication challenge before them, and develop strategies to address it. I'll suggest six routes to preparing students to discuss the climate emergency competently, assuredly, and responsibly.

The continuity of human construction of 'environment'

Just as global warming is best understood as a recent human caused aberration in the almost inconceivably long timeline of the Earth's evolution, the portrayal of environmental crisis by mass media is best situated within the portrayal by literature, over two millennia, of a changing environment and the place of humans within it. Generations before us have learned that nature is ours to dominate, amid a scattering of calls to respect and protect it (thank you Henry David Thoreau and Aldo Leopold), culminating in a climate discourse engineered largely by those who profit from environmental destruction. The title of Stauber and Rampton's 1995 critique of public relations, *Toxic Sludge is Good for You!!*, told us everything we needed to know. Warnings of environmental collapse were eloquently presented to our parents and their parents before them by writers like Rachel Carson. They choose to ignore them.

Information industries and climate destruction

The industries we prepare students for – those hiring our students (we hope), funding our departments, and perhaps employing us before we embraced the emotional, though not financial, reward of teaching – are, sadly, also leading climate villains. Let's deploy the self-reflexivity in our teaching that we encourage in our research, and be upfront with students. The products of the media and information industries have an outsized environmental footprint sitting alongside their outsized cultural footprint. The industries our students will inherit built and sustain environment destroying consumerism, while the data needs of streaming and gaming drive up the carbon footprint of everyone they entice to engage. Keilbach & Pabiś-Orzeszyna called for us to embrace 'ecocritical thinking' in our curriculum, with such topics as 'degrowth, environmental justice, and activism'. The illusion of immateriality – the sense of an industry grounded in the production of messages, not objects -

diverts attention from 'responsibility for a vast proliferation of hardware, all with high levels of built-in obsolescence and decreasingly levels of efficiency' (Boyce and Lewis, 2009, quoted in Maxwell & Miller, 2012:5). Park (2021) has recently shown us how advertising, along with digital infrastructure and journalism, exacerbate the climate emergency.

Four decades of struggle between climate journalism and forces confounding it

Veteran climate change journalists are quick to observe that the climate desk, to the extent it exists, is far from a new beat. *New York Times* science editor Walter Sullivan battled reluctant editors to put that newspaper's first major climate change story on the front page in 1981, describing increasing scientific consensus about a 'greenhouse effect'. We can ask with our students why global warming, and its inevitably disastrous outcomes, was not consistently a major global story? The answers explain much about how we define news, and where power in our industry lies.

In the 2000s, the BBC became a lightning rod for its attempts to cover climate. One BBC response to pressure from Conservative supporting UK newspapers was to become the poster child for false balance, occasionally (though never consistently) offering equal time to an energy industry representative or climate change denying politician when an expert quoting climate science was interviewed. Teachers might find it useful to provoke students to confront the absurdity of false balance by expanding their range of science reporting, perhaps asking students to report another field of science and then requiring them to find someone to deny what they discover (for example, why didn't your astronomy piece include denial that Saturn's rings are made of rock and ice?).

Understand the enemy (and its good friend, social media platforms)

As the Hackett and colleagues' climate journalism text warns us, 'the overall editorial environment favours economic growth, consumerism and private-sector business. There is little attention to who bears responsibility for climate change, and little critical analysis of capitalism or even the fossil fuel industry'. In the spirit of training effective watchdogs, we must ask students to 'follow the money' in climate change discourse. Billions of dollars – and they are, far and away, American dollars – have been spent by the energy industries and their supporters on shaping the discourse of denial, to the extent of putting almost every Republican lawmaker in the US and many hugely popular media outlets in their service. The increasing understanding that this happened while these same companies suppressed their own cutting edge climate research, and the litigation that will result for years to come, make the money trail a story in itself. But students must understand it to be prepared for the David and Goliath battle of every climate journalist.

A corollary to this theme is understanding how social media works for the enemy. Climate journalists must navigate a complex online political economy which makes climate disinformation highly profitable. The pressure group Avaaz published a study in 2020 about the role of YouTube in promoting denialism. They quote, for example, from a video titled ‘Climate Change: What Do Scientists Say?’ saying, ‘There is no evidence that CO2 emissions are the dominant factor [in climate change].’ The video is being promoted by YouTube’s algorithm and had nearly two million views by the time the report was published.

Embed climate change across the campus

My fifth theme is a callout to fellow journalism educators to strive at the institutional level to embed climate change across the curriculum. The UK National Union of Students has shown in repeated surveys that students are highly concerned about climate change and want their classes to reflect this. But they warn educators to help students to avoid debilitating levels of ‘eco-anxiety’ by becoming active agents of positive change.

Teach climate journalism strategies proven to work

Climate journalism is complicated. Old reporting strategies don’t work. Fear and doom don’t work. But people trust scientists more than journalists. Teach students how to tell their stories. People admire protesters, especially when they aren’t inconvenienced by them. Teach students how to personalise their stories. And stories about how communities are working together to solve climate challenges resonate. Advocates for a ‘solutions oriented’ journalism abound, and have good ideas for teaching the generation who will all be climate journalists helping us navigate the crisis of our times.

References

AVAAZ (2020) 'Why Is YouTube Broadcasting Climate Misinformation to Millions?'available at https://avaazimages.avaaz.org/youtube_climate_misinformation_report.pdf

Tammy Boyce and Justin Lewis (eds) (2009) *Climate change and the media*, Lausanne: Peter Lang.

Robert A Hackett, Susan Forde, Shane Gunster, and Kerrie Foxwell-Norton (2017)

'Introduction: Journalism for Climate Crisis' in *Journalism and climate crisis*, by Robert A Hackett, Susan Forde, Shane Gunster, and Kerrie Foxwell-Norton, New York: Routledge.

Judith Keilbach, and Michał Pabiś-Orzeszyna (2021) 'Green(ing) Media (Studies)', *NECSUS European Journal of Media Studies*, 10(2), pp.105-112.

Richard Maxwell and Toby Miller (2012) *Greening the media*, New York: Oxford University Press.

David J Park (2021) *Media Reform and the Climate Emergency: Rethinking Communication*

In the Struggle for a Sustainable Future, Ann Arbor: University of Michigan Press.

David Roberts (2012) 'Climate change is simple: David Roberts Ted Talk', available athttps://www.youtube.com/watch?v=A7ktYbVwr90 (Accessed 13 June)

John C Stauber and Sheldon Rampton (1995) *Toxic sludge is good for you: Lies, damn lies, and the public relations industry*, Monroe, ME: Common Courage Press.

About the contributor

Chris Paterson is Professor of Global Communication at the University of Leeds where he created undergraduate and postgraduate modules on Climate Communication. He leads a multi-year research project on climate change adaptation in rural Kenya and Ghana. He has written books about war reporting and about international news agencies, and has edited twelve anthologies and journal special issues. This chapter derives from an expert report provided for the World Journalism Education Council in 2022.

Chapter 23

Letter from Shanghai

Knowing he was visiting China, his fellow editors asked **Andrew Beck** to report back on climate change awareness there

24 September 2023

In a few minutes time I'm going to walk to Shanxi Nan Lu Metro station. The unseasonably heavy September Shanghai rain has briefly stopped. Last night it was torrential but now I can walk in the dry to take the Metro to the Pudong airport Metro station. For three years Covid, health prohibitions, travel restrictions, and prohibitively expensive air fares prevented international travel. About to leave China, I reflect on being back here for two weeks after a long absence.

Follow the paperless trail

My journey started at Hongqiao railway station. I'd bought my ticket in advance from Ctrip, the largest Chinese travel service provider. In the past I had to wait in incredibly long queues to collect my ticket. This time the Ctrip website told me that no physical ticket was necessary to gain entrance to the platform, indeed the slot into which you used to insert your ticket was now blocked. All that was needed to gain entry for Chinese nationals was their ID card, and for foreign nationals their passport. Placing my passport on the flat glass scanner at the entry barrier up popped my name and passport number as well as details of my journey - G7347 train from Shanghai Hongqiao to Hangzhou Dong, carriage 02, seat 02B – and I was through the barrier. Ahead of a train journey in the past I always used to pick up an English language newspaper from one of the Hongqiao newsstands. This time there were no newspapers and no newsstands. However, *Shine*, *Shanghai Daily* as was, was downloadable.

One hour later and the high-speed train (cruising speed 300kph) was in Hangzhou. Inside the Hangzhou Dong complex I transferred to the Hangzhou Metro, for I wasn't visiting the bustling Zhejiang capital city by the West Lake, but Xiasha, the higher education zone, to the east of the city, going to the Communication University of Zhejiang (CUZ). There to work with colleagues in the School of International Communication and Education's UK Cultural Industries research centre, my visit gave me the opportunity to meet up with an old friend, the school's deputy dean, Bao Xiaofeng. I asked him about Hangzhou's environmental policies. He started with the city's petrol vehicle policy: their licence plates limit city entry to alternate days. However, electric vehicles (EVs) can enter the city every day. In China the process of obtaining vehicle licence plates is long and tedious. Petrol vehicle owners take forever to get their plates; EV get them very quickly. Ten-year vehicle scrappage is compulsory. If a vehicle has very low mileage its life can be extended. Taxis and buses are all scrapped after ten years.

Bao offered me some historical background to the Chinese desire to save power and go green: for Chinese people, "Power sharing is in the blood". Zhejiang province used to suffer from electrical brownouts, and was an early adopter of solar power to prevent this. One aspect of President Xi's beautiful countryside project was taking remote parts of the country out of the dark with the use of solar-powered streetlights. For Bao, the Chinese positive response to climate change, the adoption of green policies, is not something novel or new; he puts it down to Chinese pragmatism. Chinese families have a sense of history, and there is a long history of doing one's best to not waste resources, to save money. Many Chinese cities also police energy consumption: not until temperatures rise to 30 degrees can air conditioning be turned on, and similar restrictions apply to heating being turned on in the winter.

Much of the CUZ campus had been taken over for use as training grounds because the 2023 Asian Games were about to take place in Hangzhou. Interviewed by reporter Zhang Meng for CGTN online on 24 August, Lu Chuan, lead director for the opening ceremony, spoke about green energy, one of the Games' themes. He added, "Hangzhou is a very special city [...] it's so green. It's one of the best places to show the whole world China wants to take the responsibility to help save the earth, to save the planet."

"No ice"

Three days later I left Hangzhou and took the HST to Changsha. Ten years or more ago I would have made this journey by air. Back then China's ageing railway network and rolling stock meant that train journeys were incredibly long and often really uncomfortable, and stations weren't always centrally located. China's HST network means that internal travel is faster, cheaper, and greener than using internal flights. Where airports are located an hour's journey from city centres, HST stations are easily accessible in downtown locations, so the four-and-a-half-hour train ride from central Hangzhou to central Changsha was soon over. I was there to meet another old friend, Professor Sun Xiangming, artist, educator, and art theorist.

The first night there we had supper with another old Changsha artist friend, Ma Jiancheng. During Covid he'd been hospitalised for two weeks, one of them in an ITU. While still evidencing reduced lung capacity he was almost his old self. Sun himself presented me with the catalogue made for an exhibition he'd had during the 2021 Hunan Design Association Design Week. Called 'South Pole and North Pole' it featured work he'd made during a 2016 Arctic visit and a 2018 Antarctic visit. The images from the South Pole were of staggeringly brutal beauty, savage landscapes of ice. Sun said that while the South Pole had been fantastic the North Pole wasn't. I asked him why, though the answer was plain to see: "No ice".

Come Saturday I took lunch with another old friend, Fu Yang. I was keen to ask him for his take on green China. He talked about both EVs and NEVs (new energy vehicles); about EV and NEV users not having to pay parking charges; about the massive increase in charge points in residential compounds for overnight charging. (China is now largest net exporter of EVs.) Moreover, lots of people see business opportunities in green energy and a cleaner environment. Lots of China unicorns are new energy companies. He explained how Beijing was trying to reduce China's reliance on fossil fuels, helping wean people off use of them, by, for example, closing coal mines in Shanxi province. But where the 1980s closure of the UK's pits was designed to punish the National Union of Mineworkers, and no help was offered to redundant miners, in China Beijing compensated miners, facilitating their relocation or retraining. When I ask him if these are examples of Chinese pragmatism, he interprets it as a manifestation of the harmonious society. A Confucian notion, the idea was revived by Hu Jintao, and became a key component in neo-Confucian thought.

"No one uses cash any more"

After lunch with Fu, I travelled with Sun, his daughter, his son-in-law, and his grandson to Dongting Hu, the huge lake in northeastern Hunan, a flood basin of the Yangtze River. We stay overnight in Yiyang city, and explore the lake in the early morning sun, but not before we'd joined some of Sun's relatives for supper. Although Yiyang city has a population of 4m, it's small by Chinese standards, and many parts have a distinctly rural feel, looking like much of China did twenty or more years ago. But even here, when it was time to pay for the meal there was no sign of paper money or credit cards; it was time to open WeChat and use WeChat Pay. One quick scan and the meal was paid for. Age seems to be no barrier to effective WeChat Pay use. As Li Zhou later remarked in Nanjing, "No one uses cash any more, even my parents".

On TV that night I tuned in to CGTN to watch *Big Story*. The magazine programme resembles *Tomorrow's World* or *Click*, and offers uniformly positive coverage of green technology innovations. Tonight's edition focused on low or no carbon impact vehicles, and featured Cake, the Swedish firm who design and make electric bikes whose carbon weight is near zero, and who aim to produce fossil-free, zero emissions bikes by 2025. As well as Cake's bikes, Candela electric, low energy consumption, fossil-free boats were featured. One model runs on a single blade, enabling the boat to rise entirely out of the water, and zip along with minimum drag. Despite some visual evidence to the contrary, there was no sense that Chinese TV was ridiculing these Scandinavians as old hippies; quite the opposite. The science is taken as a given. There is no trying to find fault. The only issue is 'how do we reduce carbon and still travel?' Not only is there a positive green culture in the Chinese population at large, but TV airtime isn't wasted with what Emily Maitlis decried in her 2022 MacTaggart Lecture as the BBC's 'both-sideism'. When Chinese TV editors have on call hundreds of respected scientists who regard climate change as a fact, they don't scrabble around trying to find one who will argue the case against.

Sustainable mobility

On Monday afternoon I travelled by HST to Nanjing to take part in three events. First was an exhibition celebrating ten years of a joint undergraduate programme between Nanjing University of Science and Technology (NJUST) and Coventry University, a course I'd had a hand in writing and which I'd helped steer through complex approval processes. None of the students had designed anything remotely resembling the gas-guzzling, boy racer vehicles of yesteryear. I was most taken by one student's design, 'Mobility for retired group to travel with their cats'. The second event was the International Design Education Forum (IDEF). All the conference papers addressed hot topics in mobility: accessibility, inclusivity, EVs, NEVs, the interconnectedness of vehicles. Moving away from fossil fuels, reducing the environmental impact of vehicles, was a given; it was not open to question. The third event was NJUST's seventieth anniversary celebration. I would have expected it to be nothing less than a terrific spectacle, and it didn't disappoint. Speeches given by distinguished international guests addressed more big issues in design. Harald Fuchs, director of the Herbert Gleiter Institute of Nanoscience at Munster University, identified three big challenges for the future: 'Decarbonisation, alternative energy sources, and health'.

Shanghai storms

A short but fast train journey had me back in Shanghai. There to attend the opening ceremony of the University of Dundee's new China office, I again took the opportunity to quiz friends old and new about China and climate change. In terms of a now paperless culture, I found my card holder with my name cards on, previously an essential in formal and informal meetings in China, never left my pocket. WeChat has completely taken over: instead of exchanging name cards, all we did was to either scan a new friend's QR code, or to offer our own QR code. I did press my case about paper. Up to a point, one friend agreed, but there's aways one place you'll find lots of paper: in bosses' offices.

After making my way in the pouring rain from the Shangjia Centre and entering the Yili Road Metro station I reflected that I must have been among the last people using paper money in Chinese cities in late 2023, and most certainly the very last one to use actual coins to ride the Metro. September has long been a popular month for business launch events in Shanghai. This unseasonably heavy rain was another prompt for climate change reflection. Granted China is one of the world's biggest polluters, but the country doesn't engage in diversionary media politics. Xi Jinping doesn't declare himself the motorist's friend, never mind the environmental damage. What's more, it is hypocritical for other, predominantly post-industrial, countries, to call out China for its record on pollution. The UK's Industrial Revolution took more than one hundred and sixty years; China's has taken barely thirty-five years. One of the key reasons air quality in the UK and the US is (relatively) good is so much heavy manufacturing has been exported to southeast Asia in general, and to China in particular. There is no earthly reason the UK or the US, with comparatively small populations, should be such mass emitters.

And with that in mind I set off home: to the post-industrial south Midlands, to a small town with some of the worst air quality in the UK, all caused by vehicle emissions and log-burning stoves. Happy trails.

Chapter 24

Letter from the Maldives

Dr Alan Geere visits an Indian Ocean paradise facing extinction through climate change and finds local journalists are fighting hard to keep the issue in the headlines

20 September 2023

Dear reader,

Greetings from Male (or Malé or Male', depending on your style book) capital of Maldives, an archipelago of atolls perched off the tip of Sri Lanka in the Indian Ocean.

I'm staying in the centre of the city and it has a lot of similarities with other places I know well, like Port of Spain in Trinidad & Tobago and Kampala in Uganda: chaotic, busy, noisy, smelly, hot, wet, full of people and traffic.

But one thing it doesn't have is drink, or more specifically alcoholic drink – and I don't miss it for a moment. As an Islamic state it is a dry country. Alcohol is not available to consume or buy. I'm told drinks can be had on the swanky resorts away from the capital. But at upwards of US$250 for a day pass, I think I'll, er, pass. There is no bar culture leading to drunks in the street, pools of vomit, fighting, bottle throwing, and the general unease that blights not just the cities but small towns across the UK.

I'm here as part of a team delivering a 'Strengthening Communications Governance' and have met courageous and industrious journalists as well as forward-thinking educators and media regulators.

Doing journalism in the Maldives

It's not the easiest of places to do journalism. There are no printed newspapers – just think about the logistics of it – so written work is published online via 'news' websites that are particularly opaque about their origins, sponsors, and commercial activity. A state TV station, Public Service Maldives, does a good job of keeping on top of government activities, while other TV outlets provide a diet of news and entertainment.

In terms of daily life, the practice of religions other than Islam is prohibited by the constitution and the religious unity law. A Hindu priest who tried to hold spiritual healing classes in Malé was arrested and deported when the Islamic minister asked the police to take action after the spiritual healing classes were advertised on social media.

The wider issues of the environment, climate change, and global issues like land use and rubbish disposal are never very far away. Most of the 1,200 coral islands grouped in a chain of 26 atolls are too small to sustain any meaningful local life and are instead populated by the exclusive (that is, expensive) resorts the country is best known for.

Climate crisis on the horizon - does anybody know?

With an average ground level elevation of just 1.5 metres above sea level, and a highest natural point of only 2.4 metres, it is the world's lowest-lying country. As a result, the Maldives are in danger of being submerged due to rising sea levels. The Intergovernmental Panel on Climate Change, the United Nations thinktank, has warned that, at current rates, sea-level rise would be high enough to make the Maldives uninhabitable by 2100.

Not that you'd know any of this by following local politics.

Reporter Shahudha Mohamed monitored the 9 September 2023 presidential election for popular online newsbrand *Dhauru* and wrote a comment piece that said: 'With the presidential election less than a month away, not a single one of the eight candidates has paid attention to climate change.'

Another environment reporter, who did not wish to be named, said one of our biggest challenges regarding environmental issues is lack of proper data and research, but no candidate proposed a way to address that either. "I feel like candidates have largely ignored the concerns raised by the general public during the past years and have failed to give climate change the focus it must be given," they said. "Even the pledges that have been made are extremely vague, such as 'will carry out development projects in a sustainable manner' and mostly focus on conservation. There has been almost no attention given to adaptation measures even though experts have warned us that the time for mitigation in Maldives have long passed and we must now be directing our valuable resources towards establishing adaptive measures."

The insider's view: grants and collaborations

For an expert view on all things environmental in the Maldives I enlisted the help of Rae Munavvar, who has worked in many sectors of the media industry for nearly a decade, from building newsrooms and selling news to teaching journalism classes across the archipelago. Best known for launching *The Edition* and her role as its first managing editor, she now works as a freelance journalist, writing for local and international outlets.

Noted for her outspokenness on matters concerning the rights of journalists, she is a passionate advocate for environment and conservation issues, and is the founder of Covering Environment, a non-profit initiative that focuses on improving eco-centric reporting across Small Island Developing State (SIDS) such as the Maldives.

Rae believes that the attitudes in the Maldives towards the environment are generally favourable. "Climate change is far too much of a reality for people to claim that weather patterns are unchanged and so forth," she says.

"However, too many journalists, particularly at the editor level, don't understand the intricacies of the climate crisis or our geographical vulnerabilities well enough to discern or translate into general reporting how multifaceted the problem is. They, therefore, may lack the ability or interest to adequately guide upcoming journalists, to whom the topic is of far more relevance, compared to the mentoring they receive in other areas."

As a result, Rae finds that otherwise capable newsrooms are not always as prepared to integrate the environmental perspective into general reporting as they could be. "In this age, environmental concerns, particularly related to climate change, interconnect everything from housing to sports and fashion, especially in the context of vulnerable SIDS. I believe these concerns must be represented across beats internationally as well as on the local front," she says.

Another issue that Rae believes they face in the Maldives is many editors tend not to grant much airtime or space to these topics. "They tend to exhaust readers – however I believe that journalists can and should pursue different avenues to counter this challenge and present stories that inspire urgent action, but in a media market that's as concentrated as ours, with a limited investor pool and battling poor economic forecasts, too often it feels like an impossible argument to win.

"Perhaps the situation could be improved through focused grants, and collaborations proposed by international news outlets - if the journalists can get more value out of it, they can advocate for their pieces, and higher-ups may be convinced to invest in the pursuit of the many, many important environmental stories that we must tell before it's too late."

Your environment correspondent writes

In search of my own environmental reporting I head to Villingili, a traffic-free island a 10-minute and 15p ferry ride from the hustle and bustle of Malé. That I even make it is partly due to the alertness of the ticket office who advised that I did not really want to go to Thilafushi, my original destination, the artificial island created 30 years ago as a municipal landfill, or 'rubbish island' in journalistic shorthand.

"That is not somewhere you would want to go," says the ticket clerk, which makes me want to go even more. But it becomes clear that a ticket will not be forthcoming so I settle for Villingili instead.

Just two kilometres from Malé, it feels a world away. There are two beaches, some shops, and a relaxed vibe, partly generated by the lack of traffic. There are plenty of boats tied up but also lots of unsightly rubbish bobbing in the blue water and some garbage on the beaches. But not as much as there could be, as I find out from Thanzy from Save the Beach, a volunteer group that has so far collected an amazing 31,416 tonnes of rubbish from the island's beaches.

"We also deal with coral restoration and rehabilitation plus community outreach, engagement, research and education," says Thanzy as she walks carefully along the beach picking up plastic bottles, cigarette cartons and food wrappers – the typical haul of rubbish collectors.

On the way back to Malé I try to envisage what 31,416 tonnes of rubbish might look like and fail miserably as the rhythmic chug of the ferry and the soporific temperature send me quietly off to another place.

But it's a lot of stuff that has been tossed aside without a care for either this world or any other world.

About the contributor

Dr Alan Geere is a journalist, editor, academic, and international editorial consultant.

EPILOGUE

Kings, queens, princes, presidents, bishops, popes, pop stars, movie stars, sports stars, business tycoons, Britain's most revered broadcaster … climate change is the issue that unites them, and turns them into global campaigners, ambassadors, and spokesmen and women. **Paul Connew** collates just a few of their most powerful, memorable messages

The king

"Just as we stand together against military aggression in Ukraine, so we must strive together to protect the world from our most existential challenge of all: that of global warming, climate change and the catastrophic destruction of nature." - King Charles III, addressing the French parliament on 21 September 2023, just 24 hours after Rishi Sunak's climate change U-turn. A coded royal rebuke?

The prince

"The Earth is the only home we have and we must think big and dream bigger if we are to protect her. The Earth is at a tipping point. We face a stark choice: either we continue as we are and irreparably damage our planet unless we remember our unique powers as humans and our continual ability to lead, innovate and problem-solve." - Prince William, announcing his Earthshot Prize finalists in New York on 19 September 2023.

The diplomat

"The era of global warming has ended; the era of global boiling has arrived. Leaders must lead. No more hesitancy. No more excuses. No more waiting for others to move. There is simply no more time for that." - UN Secretary General Antonio Guterres on 27 July 2023, after receiving two scientific reports showing global temperatures reaching their highest recorded levels in human history.

The broadcaster

"Our blind assault on the planet is changing the very fundamentals of the living world. We have over overrun the Earth. If we have not taken dramatic action within the next decade, we could face irreversible damage to the natural world and the collapse of our societies." - Sir David Attenborough, Britain's most revered broadcaster, and globally respected climate change campaigner, in his award-winning TV documentary, *Climate Change: The Fact*s.

The queen

"No one can afford to sit on the sidelines, no one can claim that climate change is somebody else's problem. Or shrug it off for future generations to address. If nations stick together, we can make fixing the climate the greatest project and the greatest achievement of our lifetime." - Queen Rania of Jordan attending the UN Climate Change summit week in New York, 21 September 2023.

The president

"The global temperature rising more than 1.5 degrees Celsius in the next two decades is scarier than nuclear war. There's no way back from that." - President Joe Biden, during a visit to Vietnam in September 2023, and after receiving the *EU Copernicus Climate Change Service* report revealing the planet had just experienced its hottest three consecutive months on record.

The tycoons

"The high-income countries have to lead the way. We have the greatest historical emissions, and we have the most risk capital and ability to innovate on these new technologies. So we not only owe it to the world to get to zero [emissions], we also owe it to them to play the primary role in driving green premiums to zero." – Bill Gates, multi-billionaire Microsoft tycoon and climate change campaigner, at a Chatham House event, London, 12 October 2023.

"The apocalypse is coming and it's coming very rapidly. I am very worried about the future [...] it won't affect me because I'll be long dead and buried." - British telecommunications billionaire John Caudwell on why he quit as the Conservative Party's biggest individual donor over Rishi Sunak's climate change 'U-turn madness' on 24 September 2023.

The Pope

"The world is nearing breaking point, some damage is irreversible […] to deny, conceal, gloss over or relativise the issue is no longer possible." - Pope Francis on 23 October 2023, criticising 'ineffectual' world leadership on climate change, and flagging up that emissions per person in the US are still double those in China.

The archbishop

"Climate change is not in itself the driver of violent conflict; however, it is a significant force-multiplier, and violent conflict is the easiest way of preventing people from taking any action on climate change by making such action impossible." – Justin Welby, Archbishop of Canterbury, addressing the House of Lords on 30 March 2023.

The movie stars

"If you do not believe in climate change, you do not believe in facts or in science or truths, climate change is real, it is happening right now, it is the most urgent threat facing our species and we need to work together and stop procrastinating." - Leonardo DiCaprio, tireless UN climate change ambassador and ecological charity founder accepting his 2016 Best Actor Oscar.

"Anyone insisting that you 'calm down' about climate change is living in denial about the catastrophes at our doorstep. Climate change is the greatest threat to our existence in our short history on this planet. Nobody is going to buy their way out of its effects." - Mark Ruffalo, Hollywood's *The Incredible Hulk* star, and activist founder of climate change/ renewable energy campaign group The Solutions Project, speaking in October 2023.

"The climate crisis poses unprecedented threats to our communities, our environment, and our security. But it won't happen as long as oil, gas, and call companies maintain their stranglehold on American politics." - Veteran Hollywood star and political activist Jane Fonda, 16 March 2022, at the launch of her Jane Fonda PAC lobby organisation, calling it the 'most important thing I do in my life'.

"I've starred in a lot of science fiction movies and, let me tell you something, climate change is not science fiction, the science is in, the debate over and the time for action is now. It is our responsibility to leave the world a better place than we found it, but right now we are failing future generations." - Arnold Schwarzenegger, *Terminator* movie star, former California governor who powerfully championed the state's groundbreaking Green Energy industrial strategy, and who now heads the Arnold Schwarzenegger Climate Change Initiative staging awareness raising events around the world.

The sport stars

"People are always talking about 2050 and how we'll do this or that, but way before that we are going to have to make big, big changes if we don't want the world to die on us." - Hector Bellerin, former Arsenal and Spain football star, and climate change campaigner who has helped fund the planting of almost 58,000 trees in the Amazon rainforest.

"We need a truly green approach in pursuit of the ultimate legacy: a safe, healthy Earth for all. We've got a relatively short window to turn climate change around and safeguard the environment for future generations." - GB international rower Melissa Wilson, in an open letter she organised to No10 Downing Street in 2020. Her co-signatories included Olympians Sir Steve Redgrave, Paula Radcliffe, Mo Farah, Rebecca Adlington, and Tessa Sanderson.

The rock star

"We spent two years consulting with environmental experts to make this tour as sustainable as possible." - Coldplay frontman Chris Martin launching their *Music of the Spheres* tour. Halfway through the tour the band had cut their CO2e emissions by nearly 50 per cent, and planted more than 5m trees, one for every ticket sold.

The influencer

But perhaps the last questioning word should go to the Swedish schoolgirl who did so much to raise climate change awareness among young people. Greta Thunberg first offered this riposte to world leaders' green platitudes at the Youth4Climate conference, Milan, Italy, 24 September 2021, and in subsequent COP-sceptic statements: "Build back better … Blah, blah, blah. Green economy… Blah, blah, blah. This is all we hear from our so-called leaders. Words that sound great but so far have not led to action. Thirty years of blah, blah, blah and where has that led us."

Printed in Great Britain
by Amazon

31670564R00141